CHARACTER EDUCATION

Grades 6–12
Year 1

by John Heidel and
Marion Lyman-Mersereau

Incentive Publications, Inc.
Nashville, Tennessee

Acknowledgments

We would like to acknowledge the many people who supported us in this project. We are indebted to these people who have given of their time and energy to help bring this project to completion.

First, we would like to name the Character Education Committee of Punahou School which conceived of the idea for this project. They set us on the right path with suggestions for what they need, as teachers, to better help in the intentional character education of our students. Special thanks to the Review Committee who offered encouragement and thoughtfully critiqued our work.

In addition, we would like to thank the many other people who provided their time and expertise in developing this complete Character Education program.

Illustrated by Marta Drayton
Cover by Bill Latta
Edited by Jennifer E. Janke

Library of Congress Catalog Card Number: 98-75493
ISBN 0-86530-429-7

TABLE OF CONTENTS

INTRODUCTION

Twenty-five hundred years ago, Socrates defined education as helping students gain both knowledge and virtue, to become both smart and good. In recent decades schools sometimes consciously and sometimes unconsciously have lost their focus on this historic mission. Now, however, educators are being called back to help children gain the virtues, the embedded habits, which constitute good character. Often those calling for character education are parents. Increasingly, they are politicians articulating the will of worried citizens. A few scholars have recognized the current lack in our schools and have become champions for character education. While these voices have been articulate in pointing out the problems of a value-neutral school or a school that rejects responsibility for character formation, these voices are limited. They lack the knowledge of and experience with the instructional issues surrounding this topic. They do not speak to the real world of schools. The authors of this book possess that knowledge and experience.

John Heidel and Marion Lyman-Mersereau have written a book that takes character education to a new level, a level that enables teachers and administrators to go beyond the abstract into that real world of their classrooms and their schools. *Character Education* is based on the authors' action research project at one of the truly lighthouse schools of our nation, the Punahou School in Hawaii.

The book reflects a complete plan for engaging a school community in the mission of character development. Central to their work and to the organization of the book is a school-wide, monthly focus on a particular virtue, such as respect or courage. In this, they are addressing one of the core problems with a school's efforts to respond to the call for character education. Americans, and particularly American educators, have frequently replaced the language of moral values and virtue with the language of psychology. Cheating is referred to as "inappropriate behavior" rather than "wrong." The goal has been "student development" and "adjustment," but development *into what* and adjustment *to what* has been left vague or unstated. This book and the program it offers educators, while on the one hand being new and fresh, returns us to an older, richer language system, one based on views of human excellence.

Over a two-year cycle, students are introduced to a deeper meaning of common words, such as loyalty, commitment and wisdom. It is here that the authors' gifts as educators become apparent. Students are not simply told the meaning of these virtue words. They are immersed in them. During the months that a particular word is being studied, each day there is a new activity which will give them greater experience and thus deeper understanding of the concept behind the word. Activities range from journal writing to a structured conversation with parents, from creating a poster about the virtue to listing ways students can practice the virtue in their everyday lives.

One of the most plaguing problems of American education is the continuing search for "the one right way": the one right way to teach reading, the one right way to evaluate student performance, the one right way to discipline students. As character education is again becoming a concern of educators, this same one-right-way mentality is becoming evident. The authors of *Character Education* take a very different approach, one that recognizes that children have very different ways of learning and that the best way to master something is to acquire it in several different learning modes. Therefore, the book offers students and teachers a rich reservoir of stories, sayings, and biographical sketches, which together bring out the depth of these concepts and show how they exist in a human life.

Character formation has been described as what we do to help students *know the good, love the good,* and *do the good.* This book addresses all dimensions of that description. The great power and benefit of *Character Education* is its appeal to the student's head, heart, and hands.

Kevin Ryan
Director of the Center for the Advancement of Ethics and Character,
Boston University

PURPOSE

Since one of the primary concerns of this program specifically relates to the total development of students, it is important to remember what a complete student is. A complete student is one who succeeds academically, but also portrays a strong moral character, with a clear sense of right and wrong.

It is probably a good exercise to reflect on how educators are doing. Most people would agree that schools across the country are doing well with academic goals and not so well with character goals. We have many students who don't know how to properly love themselves or each other, or who cheat on their schoolwork. There is teasing, gossiping, inappropriate language, and stealing. There are problems with litter and a general lack of common courtesy and good manners. We have a lot of work to do before we can fulfill the dream of a nation filled with complete students.

Thomas Lickona, developmental psychologist and author of *Educating for Character*, asserts that " . . . character must be broadly conceived to encompass the cognitive, affective, and behavioral aspects of morality. Good character consists of knowing the good, loving the good, and doing the good. Schools must help children understand the core values, adopt or commit to them, and then act upon them in their own lives."

While it might be difficult to teach values, the educational process at least can make known to students certain universal values. Students can be motivated and inspired to incorporate these values into their lives. The final step of acting out these values can be taken by giving students opportunity for community service and showing them how these values can be acted out in the community, on the playground, in the cafeteria, and in the classroom.

The purpose of this program is to design a structure whereby teachers can be more focused and intentional in their efforts to provide character education. Teachers should keep in touch with each other about activities that work, and design ways to involve parents and the wider community so the values will be reinforced. Teachers need to be conscious of who they are as role models and what values are reflected by their actions.

In all ways, our purpose is to assist teachers in their efforts to create a classroom environment where students can grow socially and spiritually, as well as intellectually. If these ideas prove useful we will be very gratified. We acknowledge the right of teachers to make this choice and to decide on their level of involvement. We know teachers enjoy autonomy, so there is room for flexibility and the development of personal style.

Much has been written about the present moral environment from which our children and youth choose their values. We know about the decline of the family, the lack of good adult models, the pervasive influence of the media, the problems of public schools, and the troubling trends in youth character. Another reason for this changing scene of morality can be traced through the gradual shift in the operative values that have characterized American life. Since the arrival of the Puritans and their lifestyle of honesty, faith, and hard work, there has been a big change. Sociologist Max Lerner made a study of American values in the mid-1950s and published his findings in *America As A Civilization* in 1957. He maintains that the idealistic values of early America became contaminated by money, materialism, competition, and success. "By the turn of the twentieth century a new pattern of life purposes emerged. Its components were success, prestige, money, power, and security." This "five-goal system" seemed to characterize the basic drives and behavioral patterns of most Americans. These five questionable values are alive and well today.

We are hopeful this program will offer other choices and have a positive impact on the daily life within each classroom and with relationships outside the classroom. This is the primary step that educators can take in reordering the moral environment of America with universal values that affirm life and enhance everyone's health and happiness. We can play an important role in the process of restoring a sense of what is right and good for our common life as Americans.

VALUE OF THE MONTH

The framework around which this project is designed is the idea of emphasizing a specific value each month. We chose eighteen values to be the featured values over a two year cycle and 36 others as supportive values. We decided on eighteen because that would give us a two-year cycle of nine values a year. This way we won't be repeating the same values each year and, with a different focus in each grade level, the values should stay fresh.

There is a specific reason for beginning with respect, following with responsibility, and leading toward compassion, faith, and commitment. It will be explained how one leads to the next and how each remains connected to all of the previous values. Some relate to seasonal themes and others become part of a total picture. However, this format is completely flexible and educators may develop their own schedule if students or current events warrant it.

VALUE OF THE MONTH BY TWO-YEAR CYCLE

In the first year students will study:

September	**Respect**	*Acceptance*	*Kindness*
October	**Responsibility**	*Self-discipline*	*Reliability*
November	**Compassion**	*Service*	*Generosity*
December	**Faith**	*Hope*	*Trust*
January	**Commitment**	*Loyalty*	*Effort*
February	**Love**	*Friendship*	*Sincerity*
March	**Wisdom**	*Knowledge*	*Understanding*
April	**Health**	*Holistic Living*	*Serenity*
May	**Humor**	*Joy*	*Enthusiasm*

In the second year, students will expand their character development by learning about:

September	**Honesty**	*Integrity*	*Truth*
October	**Cooperation**	*Family*	*Unity*
November	**Humility**	*Gratitude*	*Appreciation*
December	**Peace**	*Harmony*	*Forgiveness*
January	**Patience**	*Perseverance*	*Confidence*
February	**Courage**	*Tenacity*	*Conviction*
March	**Creativity**	*Wonder*	*Resourcefulness*
April	**Environmental Awareness**	*Beauty*	*Sacrifice*
May	**Freedom**	*Social Justice*	*Equality*

LEVELS OF FACULTY INVOLVEMENT

Basic

Aware of how busy teachers are and how much is already asked, the basic involvement is quite simple. Yet, if we accept this project as important, there is great value in everyone's involvement. It will send a clear message to the students and the wider community of the school's intention. Hopefully, there will be a general feeling of cohesion as teachers share stories about what works and as students talk about each value from their own experience.

Therefore, basic involvement would mean supporting and following the value-of-the-month idea. Specifically, it would mean posting a sign bearing the current month's value, making the students aware of it, finding a connection with your curriculum once a week, and citing an example of someone acting out that value once a week; preferably "catching a student," but also examples from the community and the world. You can take this as far as your time and interest allow; from a short announcement to a discussion.

A Little Extra

You may want to do a little extra for any of the following reasons: the value of the month goes well with your subject area or curriculum, it relates to a current event or issue within the school or worldwide, it reflects one of your concerns, or you just want to explore the possibilities a little more.

In that case, use the extensive information provided on each value in this handbook. There will be suggested activities and, where appropriate, material that will deal with specific issues such as inappropriate language, cheating or stealing. These activities will include stories, quotations, material from world religions, biographies of heroes and heroines, values in other languages, discussion questions and community service ideas. Another suggestion is to follow up a school assembly presentation with a discussion or writing assignment. This level of involvement would mean utilizing these resources two or three times a month.

Beyond the Call

Some people may become so excited about the possibilities of this program that they will use many or all of the suggested calendar activities. In that case, go for it!

Calendar

At the beginning of each month there is a calendar of suggested activities outlining a lesson plan for that month. No matter the level of involvement chosen, this calendar should help educators fit *Character Education* into their monthly routine. These calendars show daily activities which focus on the value of that month. The calendar can be used to help educators develop creative ways to teach *Character Education*. The schedule need not be followed exactly—this is only one example of how a *Character Education* lesson plan might look.

COMMENTS FROM TEACHERS

- I hope we will continue to enlarge/improve this program. Hopefully, teachers of English and perhaps social studies will have students writing on the monthly topics in character education.

- I am so pleased that Punahou has included values as an integral part of our curriculum. As an educator, there is no way I would downplay knowledge; yet as a parent and concerned adult I believe that to be truly enlightened, a person must possess clear and honorable values and a moral character.

- I can't help but feel that our focus on values has brought about a positive change in our day-to-day goings-on. Good mornings and pleases and thank-yous abounded . . .

- The *Character Education* handbook filled with guidelines and ideas for the incorporation of given values into the daily curriculum is one of the most significant steps that has taken place at Punahou . . . It resets a standard that speaks to the community at large about Punahou's stand regarding the necessity of spiritual values in daily living.

- I felt the character education program was a great success. Having the quotes in the daily bulletin and the signs in the classroom, cafeteria—everywhere—was very effective; it kept those values in the forefront of our day . . . [it] made us realize that these values were not just something to "teach" our kids, but they were ideals to be sought after by every adult on campus. In a sense they unified us. The chaplains reinforced these values in chapel programs, and the signs/values provided me and my students with a common language for our discussions of themes in our literature.

- The addition and recognition of character education as an integral part of the total curriculum of the school has been long awaited and fully embraced by all students, parents, faculty, staff and administrators alike.

- Start at the kindergarten level and continue through academy years, if not already doing so. There cannot be too much character development!

* These comments were unsolicited and were written after the first year of the program as piloted at Punahou School.

PARENTAL AND COMMUNITY INVOLVEMENT

The statement, "It takes a whole village to raise a child", refers to the community of support necessary for the upbringing of students. We acknowledge that this is not a task that educators do alone. Much of a school's success is a result of parental involvement. Parental support in reinforcing a school's educational goals for their children is imperative. We, therefore, feel it is important for parents to be aware of this particular program, so that they may more actively participate in reinforcing these goals of *Character Education*.

Through announcements, newsletters, and various other methods of communication, educators can keep parents informed of the value of the month, related activities, and opportunities to attend workshops or selected speaker engagements.

Our dreams for *Character Education* go beyond the triangle of parents, teachers, and students to include the community outside of school. As Thomas Lickona writes, the long term success of any character education depends on " . . . the extent to which families and communities join schools in a common effort to meet the needs of children and foster their healthy development."

Here are some excerpts from letters of support our project has received from parents and the community around Punahou School:

> *I am writing to applaud and commend you for attacking what I think is at the very heart of a world wide epidemic . . . During the next 1½ years, I will encourage physicians to focus on the importance of personal responsibility and other attributes of character building. I will encourage physicians to assist in spreading this message via the media and to address the community with appropriate speeches.*
> — Carl W. Lehman, M. D.
> President, Hawaii Medical Association

> *While I do teach at a Buddhist-affiliated school, the general philosophy and the values on which the Character Education program is based are universal. I will be sharing the program with all Middle School teachers and the Reverends who instruct the students in religious education.*
> — Lynette Araki
> Hongwanji Mission School

> *The Character Education program . . . is a breath of fresh air, and I encourage you . . . to vigorously continue this initiative for the sake of our children, our community, and our country.*
> — M. G. MacLaren

> *Your "village" concept has led me to conclude that we probably have more villages than we realize . . . , and, more importantly, that those villages don't communicate with each other very well. That is probably our ultimate challenge before we can really solve some of the underlying issues.*
> — Ed Case
> Representative, 23rd District, Hawaii

SUGGESTED LETTER TO PARENTS:

Dear 6–12 Parents,

This year we will be embarking on a new project in our school, a program on *Character Education.* We would like to keep you informed of our efforts in this area, since we know that "It takes a whole village to raise a child." We, as educators, are only a supplementary part of the ongoing character education in which you are involved with your child.

The values we will be teaching are among those that are universally accepted in a democratic society. As you can see from the list below, there are partner values which accompany the main value of the month. Respect and responsibility are the values for September and October. Respect and responsibility are so inclusive it is understandable why they will be taught first. They are a great foundation on which we can continue to build.

At the beginning of each month, the value being emphasized will be highlighted. We will also have a sign depicting the value of the month, partner values, and a concise definition of the main value for each classroom.

We welcome any input that you may have on our program. We are especially interested in how we can create community awareness and involvement. Thomas Lickona, author of *Educating for Character,* points out that the long-term success of any values education depends on " . . . the extent to which families and communities join schools in a common effort to meet the needs of children and foster their healthy development." The values to be taught this year are:

September	**Respect**, Acceptance, Kindness
October	**Responsibility**, Self-discipline, Reliability
November	**Compassion**, Service, Generosity
December	**Faith**, Hope, Trust
January	**Commitment**, Loyalty, Effort
February	**Love**, Friendship, Sincerity
March	**Wisdom**, Knowledge, Insight
April	**Health**, Holistic Living, Serenity
May	**Humor**, Joy, Enthusiasm

We look forward to having you join us in this worthwhile effort to continue to foster the character education which you have already begun with your children.

Sincerely,

*R*espect

SUPPORTIVE VALUES

Acceptance • Kindness

DEFINITIONS

Treating everyone including yourself with dignity.

"**Respect** means showing regard for the worth of someone or something. It includes respect for self, respect for the rights and dignity of all persons, and respect for the environment that sustains all life. Respect is the restraining side of morality; it keeps us from hurting what we ought to value." (Thomas Lickona) Mutual respect is the way we create a harmonious life with each other; respect is freely given to others and must be earned for oneself.

Acceptance is the approval of a person's worth and agreement with others' individual rights. Tolerance is often listed as an important value, but we have not included it because of the negative connotation of "putting up with someone." Acceptance goes much further. We acknowledge a person's right to disagree with us and we accept their opinion as valid.

Kindness is an expression of love and respect. Kindness puts our feelings of respect into action through words of acceptance, encouragement and support, and through acts of comfort, help and generosity.

PURPOSE

Most of the universal values and virtues that contribute to the good of the individual and society and affirm our human dignity are derived from the value of respect (and next month's value of responsibility). If we can provide our students with an understanding of these core qualities, the other values will be more quickly and easily understood. Our purpose this month is to make respect operative in the lives of our students.

Respect

September

Day One:	Day Two:	Day Three:	Day Four:	Day Five:
Discuss the meaning of the word respect.	With a partner, read and pronounce, as best you can, the word respect in other languages (see page 19). Research the cultures represented to find out ways self-respect is demonstrated in each.	Illustrate an incident in a story from pages 21-25 that demonstrates respect for a person, place or thing.	Select a proverb or maxim (page 26) that encourages self-respect. Color it and cut it out to use as a bookmark in your social studies text.	Use the statement, "Self-respect is the foundation upon which respect for others is built", as the basis for a journal entry or brief essay.
Day Six:	**Day Seven:**	**Day Eight:**	**Day Nine:**	**Day Ten:**
Rewrite a biography of a famous person whose life showed respect for others. Tell the story to a younger person you would like to influence positively.	Name: 1) a family member who demonstrates respect for good health 2) a neighbor who demonstrates respect for children 3) a community member who demonstrates respect for community property	Create and perform a cheer, complete with rhythmic movements, to celebrate respect for school helpers who work hard to make your school a pleasant place in which to learn and grow.	Design and present a "Good Example Award" to a classmate who exemplifies respect for academic excellence in a manner that sets a good example for others.	Select a hero or heroine to research (pages 28-29) and determine the influence of their respect for others in a time beyond their own life.
Day Eleven:	**Day Twelve:**	**Day Thirteen:**	**Day Fourteen:**	**Day Fifteen:**
Design a survey to determine the level of respect shown for your school's environment by its inhabitants.	Create a poster to encourage students to show respect for the school environment.	List and analyze ways students in your school demonstrate respect for their teachers.	List and analyze ways teachers and administrators in your school demonstrate respect for the students.	In small groups, compare lists made during the past two days—compare and contrast how the lists overlap.
Day Sixteen:	**Day Seventeen:**	**Day Eighteen:**	**Day Nineteen:**	**Day Twenty:**
Make a list of ways young people can show respect for the elderly in your community.	Consider ways family members can show respect for each other. Think of one specific thing you can do to increase respect in your family.	Select the service project (page 30) for demonstrating respect that you feel you could most successfully implement—make a plan for it.	Create a banner to encourage awareness of and respect for individual differences and cultural diversity in your community.	Reflect on the meaning of embracing respect for self and others as a life-shaping value.

RESPECT IN OTHER LANGUAGES

Chinese	*zun*	to honor; to venerate
	jing	to revere; to respect; to honor; reverent attention to
French	*le respect*	a state of mind which makes us treat someone or something with great esteem or consideration, e.g. respect for one's parents or respect for laws
German	*respekt*	respect, honor
Hawaiian	*ho'ihi*	treated with reverence or respect 'ihi means "sacred, holy, majestic, dignified"
Japanese	*sonkei*	to show respect by offering a glass of wine with a deep bow son -"to offer a glass of wine, or something precious or valuable" kei – "to bow by bending the body, to respect, to be discreet"
Korean	*jon kyong*	look up to with honor; venerate
Latin	*reverentia*	from Latin "respectus" (looking back, consideration, regard: from "re" (back, again) + "spicere" (to look) (something worth looking at again)
Spanish	*respeto*	respect, deference, esteem
Tagalog	*paggalang*	to feel or show honor toward others; including their ideas and property

DISCUSSION QUESTIONS

• Why is it important to be courteous to each other? Are you courteous to teachers, store clerks, people you meet, everyone?

• Why are table manners important? What are good table manners?

• What have you done in the last two days that indicates your respect for the earth?

• What are some examples of self-respect?

• Why are cleanliness, exercise, healthy eating, language, and everyday manners considered signs of self-respect?

• How is common courtesy a sign of our respect for others? What are some everyday examples?

• What are some examples of respecting the property of others? (no vandalism, no graffiti, turning in a lost wallet, taking care of something you borrow)

• What are the qualities you look for or expect from a good friend? Do these qualities describe a person who is following The Golden Rule (See page 27)?

• What are some examples of not following The Golden Rule with others, especially those who aren't our best friends? (gossip, stealing, putting others down, sarcasm)

• What are some examples from current events of people not being accepted because of their race, religion, or gender?

• Why is littering such a problem today? How can it be improved?

STORIES AND THOUGHTS FROM SPIRITUAL TRADITIONS

Christianity

"Whatsoever you wish that others would do to you, do so to them."

> – *Bible, Matthew 7:12*

"Pay all of them their dues . . . , respect to whom respect is due, honor to whom
honor is due."

> – *Bible, Romans 13:7*

"You shall not take the name of the Lord your God in vain. Honor your father
and your mother."

> – *Bible, Exodus 20:7, 12*

A Woman Washes Jesus's Feet

One of the Pharisees, Simon, asked Jesus to come to his home for lunch and Jesus accepted
the invitation. As they sat down to eat, a prostitute heard he was there and brought an
exquisite flask filled with expensive perfume. Going in, she knelt behind Jesus at his feet,
weeping, with her tears falling down upon his feet; and she wiped them off with her hair and
kissed them and poured the perfume on them.

When Simon saw what was happening and who the woman was, he said to himself, "This
proves that Jesus is no prophet, for if God had really sent him, he would know what kind of
woman this one is!"

Then Jesus spoke up and answered his thoughts. "Simon," he said, "I have something to
say to you."

"All right, Teacher," Simon replied, "go ahead."

Then Jesus told him this story: "A man loaned money to two people—$5,000 to one and
$500 to the other. But neither of them could pay him back, so he kindly forgave them both,
letting them keep the money! Which do you suppose loved him most after that?"

"I suppose the one who had owed him the most," Simon answered.

"Correct," Jesus agreed.

Then he turned to the woman and said to Simon, "Look! See this woman kneeling here!
When I entered your home, you didn't bother to offer me water to wash the dust from my feet,
but she has washed them with her tears and wiped them with her hair. You refused me the
customary kiss of greeting, but she has kissed my feet again and again from the time I first
came in. You neglected the usual courtesy of olive oil to anoint my head, but she has covered
my feet with rare perfume. Therefore, her sins—and they are many—are forgiven, for she
loved me much; but one who is forgiven little, shows little love."

Character Education Year 1 Grades 6–12

And Jesus said to her, "Your sins are forgiven."

Then the men at the table said to themselves, "Who does this man think he is, going around forgiving sins?"

And Jesus said to the woman, "Your faith has saved you; go in peace."

– Bible, Luke 7:36-50

Islam

God's rebuke to Adam for scorning Iblis

> To whomsoever God's order comes,
> He must smite with his sword even his own child.
> Fear then, and revile not the wicked,
> For the wicked are impotent under God's commands.
> In presence of God's commands bow down the neck of pride.
> Scoff not nor chide even them that go astray!
> One day Adam cast a look of contempt and scorn
> Upon Iblis, thinking what a wretch he was.
> He felt self-important and proud of himself,
> And he smiled at the actions of cursed Iblis.
> God Almighty cried out to him, "O pure one,
> Thou art wholly ignorant of hidden mysteries.
> If I were to blab the faults of the unfortunate,
> I should root up the mountains from their bases,
> And lay bare the secrets of a hundred Adams,
> And convert a hundred fresh Iblises into Musulmans."
> Adam answered, "I repent me of my scornful looks;
> Such arrogant thoughts shall not be mine again.
> O Lord, pardon this rashness in Thy slave;
> I repent; chastise me not for these words!:
> O Aider of aid-seekers, guide us,
> For there is no security in knowledge or wealth;
> "Lead not our hearts astray after Thou hast guided us,:
> And avert the evil that the "Pen" has written.
> Turn aside from our souls the evil written in our fates,
> Repel us not from the tables of purity!

– Teachings of Rumi p 58-60

The best of you is he who is the best to his people.*

* or wife

– Selections from Mishkat-ul-masabi [386] p 87
'A'ishah, TI

He who is devoid of kindness is devoid of (all) good.

> *— Selections from Mishkat-ul-masabi [380] p 86*
> *Jarir, MU*

Verily, it is of the best (parts) of goodness for a man to be good to those who bore love to his parent after that [sic] he (or she) is gone.

> *— Selections from Mishkat-ul-masabi [388] p 88*
> *Ibni 'Umar, MU*

Chinese

"A young man's duty is to behave well to his parents at home and to his elders abroad, to be cautious in giving promises and punctual in keeping them, to have kindly feelings towards everyone, but seeks the intimacy of the Good." — *Confucius*

"In the presence of a good man, think all the time how you may learn to equal him. In the presence of a bad man, turn your gaze within." — *Confucius*

"The wise man seeks to restrain the actual needs of the people, not to excite them by the sight of luxuries. The esteem of things brings covetousness and disorder." — *Lao Tzu*

"There is no evil worse than ambition; no misery worse than discontent; no crime greater than greed. Content of mind is peace and satisfaction eternal." — *Lao Tzu*

Tzu-Chin said to Tzu-kung, when our Master arrives in a fresh country he always manages to find out about its policy. Does he do this by asking questions, or do people tell him of their own accord? Tzu-kung said, our Master gets things by being cordial, frank, courteous, temperate, deferential. That is our Master's way of inquiring—a very different matter, certainly from the way in which inquiries are generally made. — *The Analects, Book 1*

Tzu-yu asked about the treatment of parents. The Master said, Filial sons nowadays are people who see to it that their parents get enough to eat. But even dogs and horses are cared for to that extent. If there is no feeling of respect, wherein lies the difference?

Men do not like to be fatherless, virtueless, unworthy; yet rulers describe themselves by these names. Thus increase brings decrease to some, and decrease brings increase to others. Others have taught thus; I consent to it. Violent men and strong die not by natural death. This fact is the foundation of my law. — *Tao Te Ching*

What shall it profit a man if he gain fame or wealth, and lose his life? If a man clings to fame or wealth, he risks what is worth more. Be content, not fearing disgrace. Act not, and risk not criticism. Thus live long, without alarm. — *Tao Te Ching*

India

The Disbeliever

LONG ago there were two friends, two young men of the same age and occupation, who, although they were devoted friends, were always quarreling.

The trouble was that whereas one of them was a believer, the other was a confirmed atheist, and consequently the arguments they would have over whether God existed or not often became quite fierce.

One day a dreadful thing happened.

They went off to work as usual, which was cutting down trees for firewood, when again they began to argue.

"I tell you there is a God," said the believer.

"Nonsense," smiled the other cynically.

"There must be a God, I tell you, because in the first place we didn't create ourselves, did we? And in the second place, nothing can come from nothing . . . "

"Oh, fiddlesticks," said the disbeliever calmly, "it's poor fools like you who believe everything they are told because they have no sense to think for themselves. Now if you had read as much as I have on the subject . . . "

Suddenly his friend lost his temper completely.

"There is a God, I tell you," he screamed, and raising the axe he was carrying brought the blunt end crashing down on his friend's head, killing him outright and raising a bump.

Then horrified and full of remorse at what he had done, he hit himself on the head and slumped down dead beside the body of his companion.

Presently they both stood, sadly looking down at the mortal frames they had so violently vacated, for they were now in their subtle bodies.

But habit dies hard, and when they realized they weren't at all dead, they began to argue again.

"Now look what you've done," complained the agnostic. "You had no right to hit me with the hatchet."

"I was merely trying to impress upon you," said the other patiently, "the undeniable fact that there is a God."

"That's all very well, but you could have been a little more tactful."

Just then a holy man came upon the scene and, seeing the two youthful bodies lying there, began to weep in pity. Solemnly he began to pray that life be again restored to those two bodies that had been so cruelly struck down in the prime of youth. And so earnest were his entreaties that two gods came down in response.

The gods looked at the bodies, and observing that they were young and fresh and, apart from the bumps, almost as good as new, they decided that they would themselves inhabit them, and go a-romping about the earth for a while. Whereupon the holy man was overjoyed to see his prayer answered, for the bodies came to life, stood up, turned to each other and smiled, then hand in hand joyfully went on their way.

"There," exclaimed the believer triumphantly, "I told you there was a God."

"Oh fiddlesticks," said the agnostic calmly, "it's poor fools like you who believe everything they see. Now if you had read as much as I have on the subject . . . "

But his companion wasn't listening any more. He was reaching for the axe again.

Judaism

The Rabbi's Gift

There was a monastery which had fallen on hard times. At one time its buildings had been filled with young monks, and its big church had resounded with the singing of the chant. Only a handful of old monks were left in the decaying mother house, the abbot and four others. Clearly this was a dying order.

In the deep woods surrounding the monastery there was a little hut, which a rabbi had built, and to which, from time to time, he would go to fast and to pray. The monks had become a bit psychic from their years of quiet contemplation and prayer, and they could sense when the rabbi was at his hermitage. They would whisper among themselves, "The rabbi walks in the woods."

Agonizing over the imminent death of his order, the abbot decided to visit the rabbi at his hut, hoping that he might offer some advice that could save the monastery. The rabbi welcomed the abbot at his hut with open arms. The abbot explained the purpose of his visit, and the rabbi empathized with him, replying that it was the same in his town—the spirit seemed to have left the people, and almost no one went to the synagogue anymore. The old rabbi and the old abbot wept together, then they read the Torah together and spoke of deep and profound things. "It has been a wonderful thing that we could meet after all these years," said the abbot, "but please, can you give me some advice that might help save my dying order?"

"I am sorry," replied the rabbi, "I have no advice for you. All I can tell you is that the Messiah is one of you."

The abbot returned to the monastery where the monks questioned him, asking what advice the rabbi had given him. The abbot told them what the rabbi had said, that the Messiah was one of them.

In the months that followed, the monks pondered this idea and wondered what the significance of the rabbi's words could be. "The Messiah is one of us? Could he possibly mean one of us monks right here in this monastery? Well then, which one of us? He probably meant the Father Abbot. Yes, he has been our leader for so long. But then again he might have meant Brother Thomas. He is truly a holy man, a man of light. He couldn't have meant Brother Phillip. Brother Phillip is so crotchety at times and is a thorn in people's sides. Yet when you think about it, Phillip always seem to do and say the right thing at the right time. What about Brother Daniel? No, Brother Daniel is so passive, a real nobody. But then he has a gift for somehow always being there when you need him. Maybe Daniel is the Messiah. Of course the rabbi couldn't mean me. He couldn't possibly mean me. I'm just an ordinary person. Yet what if he did? Could I mean that much to God?"

As they thought about each other in this way, they began to treat each other with a very special reverence on the off chance that one of them might be the Messiah. There was a gentle, wholehearted, human quality about them which was hard to describe but easy to notice.

Visitors to the beautiful forest near the monastery would often picnic on their lawn and wander along its paths. They were deeply moved by the life of these monks. Before long, people were coming from far and wide to be nourished by the atmosphere of the place, which was strangely attractive, even compelling, and once again young men were asking to become part of the community. Within a few years the monastery had become a thriving order, and although the rabbi no longer walked in the woods, thanks to his gift, it was a vibrant center of light and spirituality in the realm.

Character Education Year 1 Grades 6–12

PROVERBS AND MAXIMS

Wherever there is a human being, there is an opportunity for kindness.

— *Seneca*

It is the weak who are cruel. Gentleness and kindness can only be expected from the strong.

— *Leo Rosten*

Kindness is the golden chain by which society is bound together.

— *Goethe*

Wise sayings often fall on barren ground; but a kind word is never thrown away.

— *Arthur Helps*

Kindness gives birth to kindness.

— *Sophocles*

THE GOLDEN RULE THROUGH THE AGES

Zoroastrianism

That nature alone is good which refrains from doing unto another whatsoever is not good for itself.   *– Zoroaster, 6th century B.C.E.*
Dadistan-i-dimik, 94,5

Buddhism

Hurt not others with that which pains thyself.   *– Buddha, 6th century B.C.E.*
Udana Varga, 5,18

Taoism

Regard your neighbor's gain as your own gain, and your neighbor's loss as your own loss.   *– Tai Shang Kan Ying P'ien*

Confucianism

Is there one maxim which ought to be acted upon throughout one's life? Surely it is the maxim of loving-kindness: Do not do unto others what you do not want others to do unto you.   *– Confucius, 6th century B.C.E.*
The Analects 15, 23

Greek Philosophy

May I do unto others as I would that they should do unto me.   *– Plato, 5th century B.C.E.*

Hinduism

This is the sum of duty: Do naught unto others which would cause you pain if done to you.   *– from the Mahabarata, 3rd century B.C.E.*

Judaism

What is hateful to you, do not to your fellowman. That is the entire law; all the rest is commentary.   *– Talmud, Shabbat 3id.*

Do not do unto others what thou wouldst not they should do unto thee.   *– Rabbi Hillel, 1st century B.C.E.*

Christianity

Do unto others as you would have others do unto you. *– Jesus, 1st century C.E.*

Islam

None of you is a believer until he desires for his brother that which he desires for himself.   *– Muhammed, 6th century C.E.*
Sunnah

Baha'i

Lay not on any soul a load which ye would not wish to be laid upon you and desire not for anyone the things you would not desire for yourself.   *– Baha'ulla, 19th century C.E.*

HEROES AND HEROINES

BENAZIR BHUTTO (1953–)

Born in Karachi, Pakistan, as the oldest daughter of Zulfikar Ali Bhutto, a Pakistani political leader and a follower of the Sunnite branch of Islam, and Begum Nusrat Bhutto, daughter of an Iranian merchant that followed the Shi'ite Moslem tradition, Benazir Bhutto was educated in a Roman Catholic convent school and entered Radcliffe College in the United States at age 16. Returning to Pakistan, she became a strong supporter of her father as well as a political activist. For her efforts and her pleas for political freedom and justice, she spent most of the time between 1977 and 1986 in detention, in jail or under house arrest. She served for a time as President of Pakistan and continues to struggle for social reform and equality for the people of Pakistan.

ABRAHAM LINCOLN (1809–1865)

Born in a log cabin on a farm in Hardin County, Kentucky, Lincoln grew tall and strong from his work on the frontier. He also grew strong in character and was first noticed by the public when he was placed in charge of a small mill and store. He became skilled as a wrestler, debater, military leader and politician. As the sixteenth president of the United States and president during the Civil War, Lincoln was immortalized by his Emancipation Proclamation, his Gettysburg Address, and two outstanding inaugural addresses. He had never learned to hate, and throughout his presidency was committed to restoring the union and freeing the slaves. He respected his enemies and modeled understanding, forgiveness, and kindness.

GOLDA MEIR (1898–1978)

Born in Kiev, Ukraine, she emigrated with her family to Milwaukee, Wisconsin in 1906. She attended a local teachers' college and taught in the public schools until 1921, at which time she left for Palestine and joined Kibbutz Merchavia. She became active in the World Zionist Organization in 1929 and participated in several Jewish agencies and councils. She served as Israel's foreign minister from 1956-1966 and prime minister from 1969-1974. She was a pioneer in struggles leading to the creation of a Jewish state and is described as one of the great women in Jewish history. She was instrumental in securing general peace agreements with Arab nations in the early 1970s.

SHINRAN (1173–1262)

Born in Kyoto, he was a member of the illustrious Fujiwara family, which ruled Japan during the Heian period. He was orphaned at an early age and entered a monastery near Kyoto, where he began an intense study of Tendai Buddhism. He found this unsatisfying and became a disciple of Honen, founder of Jodo, or The Pure Land School. Shinran developed the beliefs of Jodo to its simplest form in order to reach all levels of people. Other established branches of Buddhism regarded his stance as subversive because of its emphasis on the common person, its egalitarian viewpoint, and its simple, individualistic approach to deliverance. Though Shinran was not well-known during his own day, his teachings were known as Jodo Shinoku and became one of the largest Buddhist denominations as well as the major tradition of those Japanese who immigrated to America during the end of the 19th century.

ROGER WILLIAMS (ca. 1603–1683)

Born in London, educated at Cambridge, chaplain to Sir William Masharn of Essex in 1629, Williams became disenchanted with the Anglican Church and sailed for Massachusetts with his wife in 1630. He was banished from Massachusetts in 1635 because he taught that churches in the colonies had not "separated" themselves from the corrupt Anglican Church. In spite of these conservative views, he believed that all men have the same natural rights and should share land equally; he assisted in setting up a democratic land association. He was a champion of the rights of Native Americans and supported the separation of Church and State. He also supported, while disagreeing with, the beliefs of other religious groups such as Quakers and Jews.

PUT RESPECT INTO ACTION

- Practice The Golden Rule.

- Practice Random Acts of Kindness.

- Support someone who receives a "put down."

- Make an effort to not swear.

- Object when someone wants to deface or destroy public or private property.

- Listen to someone who disagrees with you and respect their opinion.

- Practice sincerity in your conversations; eliminate sarcasm and untruthfulness.

COMMUNITY SERVICE IDEAS

- Entertain senior citizens at a retirement home; taking them small gifts, singing to them, talking with them.

- Correspond with students from another country and learn about each other's culture.

- Write letters of appreciation to community leaders.

- Volunteer with the Library for the Blind and Physically Handicapped.

- Volunteer with Ronald McDonald House; housekeeping, landscaping, baking cookies, or office work.

- Survey your school to investigate facilities for handicapped students and visitors. Make recommendations for improvements and conduct a fund-raiser to support those changes.

- Select another school in your community and share with them the meaning of respect. Exchange art projects, school calendars, original writings and note and discuss similarities and differences. Try to exchange visits.

BOOKS ON RESPECT

An Angel for Solomon Singer. Cynthia Rylant. New York: Orchard Books, 1992.

The Big Orange Splot. Daniel Manus Pinkwater. New York: Hastings House, 1977.

Fish is Fish. Leo Lionni. New York: Pantheon Books, 1970.

From the Mixed-up Files of Mrs. Basil E. Frankweiler. Elaine Konigsburg. New York: Atheneum, 1967.

Gentle Hands. M.E. Kerr. New York: Viking Press, 1975.

The Hundred Penny Box. Sharon Bell Mathis. New York: Viking Press, 1975.

The Rare One. Pamela Rogers. Nashville: Thomas NElson, Inc., 1974.

Rosie the Cool Cat. Pitor Wilkon. New York: Viking, 1991.

Sea Glass. Laurence Yep. New York: HArper & Row, 1979.

The Story of Abraham Lincoln. Ann Donegan Spencer. La Jolla: Value Communications, Inc., 1977.

The Story of Elizabeth Fry. Spencer Johnson. La Jolla: Value Communications, Inc., 1976.

Throwing Shadows. Elaine Konigsburg. New York: Atheneum, 1979.

Watch Out for the Feet in Your Chicken Soup. Tomie dePaola. Englewood Cliffs: Prentice-Hall, 1974.

The Book of Virtues. William J. Bennett, ed. New York: Simon and Schuster, 1993.

   "Letter from Birmingham City Jail" – p. 258

   "Lincoln's Second Message to Congress" – p. 256

A Call to Character. Colin Greer and Herbert Kohl, eds. New York: Harper Collins Publishers, 1995.

   "All Things Bright and Beautiful" – p. 258

   "Among the Tribes" – p. 308

   "The Diary of Anne Frank" – p. 292

   "Invisible Man" – p. 293

   "The Lion, The Witch, and the Wardrobe" – p. 260

A 4th Course of Chicken Soup for the Soul. Jack Canfield, "etal." Deerfield Beach: Health Communications, 1997.

   "The Small Gift" – p. 312

The Moral Compass. William J. Bennett, ed. New York: Simon and Schuster, 1995.

   "The Legend of Saint Christopher" – p. 710

   "The Life Heroic" – p. 360

Responsibility

SUPPORTIVE VALUES

Self-discipline • Reliability

DEFINITIONS

Taking care of your duties and answering for your actions.

Responsibility means being accountable or answerable to something within one's power. Thomas Lickona calls this the active side of morality. "It includes taking care of self and others, fulfilling our obligations, contributing to our communities, alleviating suffering, and building a better world." (Lickona)

Self-discipline is the disciplined training of one's self with some form of self-improvement in mind. This is a trait used by athletes, artists and musicians and should be used by students in the same way. There is also an important underlying theme of self-control. For personal happiness and social harmony we need to act and speak appropriately.

Reliability means that we can be counted on to follow through on all our responsibilities; our word is trustworthy, we are dependable in achievement, accurate in our assessments and honest in all our dealings.

PURPOSE

Along with respect, responsibility is a core value under which fall several other themes. The emphasis for this month will center on accountability and dependability. Since so many other values relate to respect and responsibility, success in making them understood depends on how well these first two are learned. The goal is to make respect and responsibility central character traits within the lives of all students.

Responsibility — October

Day One:
Discuss the meaning of the word responsibility and its impact on one's personal value system.

Day Two:
Work in small groups to brainstorm and quickly list words that "come into your head" as having a similar meaning as responsibility.

Day Three:
Create a word find or crossword puzzle with the "similar meaning" word lists generated yesterday.

Day Four:
Exchange and work the puzzles—share copies of word lists and complete puzzles with the entire group.

Day Five:
Select a proverb or a maxim (page 43) that might serve as a reminder to you of the need for developing goals and daily habits to reinforce a high level of personal responsibility. Write it in a permanent place in your notebook.

Day Six:
In a group setting, distribute and discuss copies of the word responsibility in other languages (page 35), with an emphasis on gaining better understandings of the cultures represented.

Day Seven:
Write a journal entry or brief essay critiquing the level of responsibility you feel you exhibit through your behavior for the health and well being of your classmates and friends. Name some specific things you do or do not do.

Day Eight:
Ponder the importance and implications of family members' responsibility to and for each other. Cite examples of positive role models in history, literature, and within your own community.

Day Nine:
How much responsibility do you feel you have for a clean and litter-free school environment? Prepare a letter to the editor or radio talk show justifying your position.

Day Ten:
List the personal traits necessary for a person to exhibit responsible leadership. Consider the consequences of persons without these traits who occupy positions of power.

Day Eleven:
List the name of the person or persons in your school who are responsible for 1) Student Safety 2) Integrity of the athletic program 3) Attention to Academic Excellence and 4) Codes of Ethics and Moral Conduct. Define your understanding of what these people are responsible for.

Day Twelve:
What measures are in place in your school to deal with acts of student responsibility related to community property and school rules? Prepare a five minute speech to present your evaluation of the effectiveness of these measures.

Day Thirteen:
Think of (or search through song books) for a song that inspires citizens of your country to accept responsibility for the good of the country and its citizens. Write a new verse for the song.

Day Fourteen:
Develop a bill of rights for children that outlines parents major responsibilities to their children.

Day Fifteen:
Create an illustrated poster to promote awareness of and respect for children's responsibility to their parents.

Day Sixteen:
Consider the following: "young people of today do not feel responsibility for the well being of the elderly as did young people of generations past." Take a position and justify, in some creative manner, what you think about this statement.

Day Seventeen:
Should people of your age feel a responsibility for 1) homeless and hungry people, 2) world peace, 3) law and order in the community? Justify your answers and tell what, if anything, you can do to meet these responsibilities.

Day Eighteen:
Elaborate on the well-known and much-quoted saying "a penny saved is a penny earned" as it applies to financial responsibility. Define "good stewardship" in your own words.

Day Nineteen:
Write a creative story, poem, play, song or rap about an irresponsible act that resulted in group consequences to people other than the person performing the act—give your creation a happy ending by allowing the unfortunate character to atone for and correct the irresponsibility.

Day Twenty:
Reflect on the impact on one's major life decisions through embracing responsibility as a core value.

RESPONSIBILITY IN OTHER LANGUAGES

Chinese	*zé*	duty; responsibility; to lay charge upon; to upbraid; to ask from; to demand
	ren	an official position; an office; to employ; to put in office
French	*la responsibilité*	the ability to make a decision without the need to have the approval of a higher authority; obligation one has to make up for a mistake, fulfill a duty or a commitment
German	*verantwortung*	to answer for, to account for, to defend, to vindicate; accept the reasons for being accountable
Hawaiian	*kuleana*	right, privilege, concern, responsibility
Japanese	*sekinin*	to condemn someone to carry a heavy task on that person's back seki – to press a person for payment, to condemn, to blame nin – to carry a heavy thing on one's back
Korean	*chaek im*	accountable for a given task
Latin	*cura*	from Latin "re" (back) + "spondere" (to pledge)
Spanish	*responsubitidad*	responsibility, liability, accountability
Tagalog	*katungkulan*	to take care of one's tasks, duties, debts, and, especially, children

DISCUSSION QUESTIONS

• What are appropriate exclamations for anger or pain or surprise?

• What are situations when self-control is difficult?

• How have your responsibilities changed in the last four years? Do you consider the new responsibilities fair?

• Are you considered dependable by your friends? By your family? Why or why not?

• Do you always follow through on your responsibilities?

• Do you consider yourself a disciplined person?

• How difficult is it to get yourself moving toward fulfilling your responsibilities?

• Where does discipline come from? How can you improve?

• Why are adults concerned about the language used by people of your age? Do they have a strong case? How aware are you of your own language? Is this an issue of self-control?

STORIES AND THOUGHTS FROM SPIRITUAL TRADITIONS

Hinduism

Whatever a great man does, ordinary people will imitate; they follow his example. Consider me: I am not bound by any sort of duty. There is nothing in all the three worlds, which I do not already possess; nothing I have yet to acquire. But I go on working, nevertheless. If I did not continue to work untiringly as I do, mankind would still follow me, no matter where I led them. Suppose I were to stop? They would all be lost.

> The ignorant work
> For the fruit of their action:
> The wise must work also
> Without desire
> Pointing man's feet
> To the path of his duty
>
> Let the wise beware
> Lest they bewilder
> The minds of the ignorant
> Hungry for action:
> Let them show by example
> How work is holy
> When the heart of the worker
> Is fixed on the Highest.

— Bhagavad Gita

With power comes responsibility. The more the power, the greater the responsibility. If one obtains the former and doesn't fulfill the latter, then that person will sure be reborn in a hell realm.

— Tradition

Buddhism

We are responsible for the actions (karma) we create through our body, speech, and mind. This is the law of cause and effect: we reap the fruits of the seeds we plant. If we plant mango seeds, we reap mangos. If we plant chili seeds, we reap chilies. If we don't plant mango, we can never expect to reap mangos. If we don't plant chili seeds, we need not worry about reaping chilies.

Our life is our own personal responsibility. And human life is very precious. As human beings we have enough suffering to know we want to avoid it. We have enough pleasure to know we like it. We have intelligence to discriminate between wholesome actions and unwholesome actions. We can hear, speak, and engage in spiritual practice. As a human, we have maximum potential for spiritual growth.

But achieving a human rebirth is not as easy as it may seem. Imagine a vast ocean, as boundless as the sky. And upon this great ocean floats a golden yoke, buffeted to and fro by the winds and the waves. Underneath the ocean lives a blind turtle, who floats up to the surface of the ocean once every hundred years. Because of the unwholesome actions we have created, the chances of being reborn as a human being are the same as the chances of the blind turtle putting his head through the golden yoke.

We are each accountable for our own actions. As human beings we have the chance to purify our mind, purify our karma, and do good deeds. Reflecting that life is short, and the end can come at any time, we should turn from worldly activities and devote our energies to spiritual pursuits.

Buddhism teaches us to take responsibility not only for ourselves, but also for others. We come to understand that all living beings are interdependent. We reflect on the help we receive from countless beings, beginning from our birth. Without our mother's loving care, as a baby we couldn't have survived for even a day. Even the lunch on our table represents the combined efforts of hundreds of people. When we get seriously ill, we are completely helpless, totally dependent on physicians and the loving care of family and friends. Contemplating like this, we realize that we have a responsibility for each other. We realize the importance of developing what His Holiness Dalai Lama calls "a sense of universal responsibility."

Recognizing the kindness we have received from others throughout our life (and past lives), we generate a sense of gratitude. Remembering others' kindness, we send forth the wish, 'May all beings be happy! May they all be free from suffering!' Next, we acknowledge that simply wishing happiness for others, as virtuous and beneficial as it may be, is not enough. It is important to act on these fine sentiments and take action to bring them happiness and alleviate their sufferings. We cannot in good conscience leave this task to others. Moved by great compassion, we realize how important it is that we personally take on the responsibility, called "the extraordinary intention," that gives rise to the altruistic, enlightened state of mind.

Once there was a monk who practiced meditation in solitude in a mountain cave. One day a woman suddenly appeared and falsely accused him of being the father of her child. Angrily, she thrust the boy forward, saying, "Take him, he's yours." The monk took the boy without a word and lovingly raised him as his own son.

Twelve years later, when the boy got big enough to work, the woman suddenly appeared again. "Where is my son?" she demanded. "Give my son back to me." Without saying a word, the monk brought the child and gave him back to his mother.

Islam

Islam is a religion of Faith in Practice. We do not relegate our beliefs to a sacred building or a special day. They are the way we live our lives. As Muslims, it is incumbent on us to act on behalf of Righteousness. Evil deeds may necessitate we act within the third area of punishment in Islamic law, which is meted out according to discretion. It may simply be a box around the ears or it may mean going into battle. If we cannot change an evil practice through action, we should at least voice our disapproval; and if this has no effect then we should at least hope and pray that it changes. We fail ourselves and Allah if we begin by hoping and praying but go no further.

The Essential Teachings of Islam: Daily Readings from the Sacred Texts p 230-1 354:
Hadith Muslim: (An-Nawawi's Forty Hadith)

Hawaii

The Oyster of Pu'uloa

A long time ago, a great lizard brought a special kind of oyster to Hawaii from far away Tahiti and planted them in Pu'uloa, what is now known as Pearl Harbor. In the kapu protected harbor they grew and multiplied. Kapu meant that there were only certain times of the year that you could gather these oysters from this area. In this way they could grow and provide food for many people.

One day, a woman was gathering seaweed in her basket. As she wandered, pulling little bits of seaweed here and there, she put her hand into a hole and felt an oyster. She looked around to see if anyone was near, since she knew that the oysters were kapu or forbidden at this time of year. She took the oyster and hid it under the seaweed in her basket and continued looking for oysters, which she loved to eat. When the woman was finished with her gathering, the overseer of the area came to check her basket. She told him that she only had seaweed. He took her basket to see for himself and discovered the oysters. "You have broken the kapu!" he yelled angrily. "You shall be punished." And he took her basket and threw all that she had gathered back into the ocean and then pulled her basket apart. "Now you must leave without anything."

The woman knew she was wrong and that she deserved punishment. She was ashamed of what she had done and walked home feeling very unhappy. The overseer followed her and

Character Education Year 1 Grades 6–12

soon confronted her. "You must give me money," he commanded. "You broke the kapu and this is part of your punishment."

The poor woman felt she had been punished enough and refused the man, but he insisted that she pay. She finally gave him all the money she had, which was only a single coin. The great lizard was very angry at all that she had seen, for she did not believe the woman deserved to be punished twice. In her anger, she took all of the pearl oysters, which she had brought to the harbor, and planted them back in Tahiti, which is now famous for pearls. Because of the irresponsible woman and the overseer, there are no longer any pearls in Pearl Harbor.

Pueblo Indian

The Story of Crow and Hawk

Once there was a beautiful black crow. She had a nest on the side of a rocky hillside. She was quite proud of it as it was full of eggs. There she sat waiting for her eggs to hatch. She sat and sat, but nothing happened. She sat some more and still, nothing happened. Finally, Crow got tired of all that sitting, and she just flew away.

The eggs sat in the nest unguarded. They sat and sat, but Crow did not return. After a while, a lovely Hawk flew by. She swooped once over the nest, spotting the eggs. Again she swooped over the nest trying to spot the mother bird. The third time she swooped over the nest she said to herself, "The mother of these eggs no longer cares for them. Poor little eggs. I shall sit on them until the mother returns."

Hawk sat on the eggs. She sat and sat, but nobody came. For days she sat, guarding and warming Crow's eggs. Then one day, the eggs began to hatch. Little black crows began to chip and push their way out of their shells. They chirped and called for their mother, but no crow came. Hawk looked down at them tenderly and said, "I will care for you, little ones." She flew about to find food for them, and when she returned she watched over them. Day after day, she fed them and looked after them.

The tiny crows grew bigger with Hawk's food and care. Their beautiful black feathers grew glossy and their wings grew strong. Still Hawk cared for them and fed them well.

Carefree Crow was flying over her old home on the hillside one day and spotted the nest she had left so long ago. "Perhaps I should return to it," she thought. As she approached the nest, she saw Hawk taking care of the little crows. "How dare you, Hawk!" screeched Crow, swooping down to the nest. "What's wrong?" asked Hawk, quite surprised. "Don't you know? I want my little crows back! They're mine!" screamed the very excited Crow.

Hawk ruffled her feathers and for a moment, was silent. Then she spoke softly, but firmly. "It is true, you laid the eggs. I see now that they were yours. But you flew off and left them, untended and unguarded. Anything could have happened to those poor little eggs. But I saw them and came to sit on the nest. For days I did not leave them. For days I did not eat a thing. When they hatched, I worked hard to find them food so that they would grow strong. It is I who have cared for them. It is I who will keep them!"

"I want them back!" screeched Crow once more.

"You may not have them," said Hawk. "Where were you when they needed warmth? Where were you when they were hungry? It is too late for you to come back now. They will stay with me."

"Well then," snapped Crow, "I will go to the King of the Birds and see what he has to say about this!"

"A fine idea." Hawk agreed and off they went to see Eagle.

When they had told Eagle the story, Eagle asked, "Why did you leave your nest, Crow?"

Crow said nothing. Eagle turned to Hawk. "And how did you, Hawk, come upon the eggs?" asked Eagle.

"I was out flying one day when I saw a nest full of eggs with no one sitting on it. I waited to see if someone would come, but no one came at all." replied Hawk.

"But I laid those eggs!" cried Crow.

"Yes, but you did not care for them. It was I who sat on the eggs. It was I who hatched them and it was I who fed the little birds," said Hawk.

"But I am their mother! Just ask them. Go on and ask the little ones who their mother is!" said crow.

"Well," said Eagle turning to the baby birds, "who is your mother then?"

All together the little birds chirped, "Hawk is the only bird we call mother."

"No, I am your real mother," protested Crow.

But the little birds chorused, "You left us. Hawk stayed to hatch us and feed us. She is the only mother we know."

And so, it was settled. The little crows would stay with Hawk and not with Crow. And that is how precious things are lost when they are neglected.

Christianity

Responsibility is Rewarded

. . . the Kingdom of Heaven can be illustrated by the story of a man going into another country, who called together his servants and loaned them money to invest for him while he was gone.

He gave $5,000 to one, $2,000 to another, and $1,000 to the last—dividing it in proportion to their abilities—and then left on his trip. The man who received the $5,000 began immediately to buy and sell with it and soon earned another $5,000. The man with $2,000 went right to work, too, and earned another $2,000.

But the man who received the $1,000 dug a hole in the ground and hid the money for safekeeping.

After a long time, their master returned from his trip and called them to him to account for his money. The man to whom he had entrusted $5,000 brought him $10,000.

His master praised him for good work. "You have been faithful to me in handling this small amount," he told him. "So now I will give you many more responsibilities. Begin the joyous tasks I have assigned to you."

Next came the man who had received the $2,000, with the report, "Sir, you gave me $2,000 to use, and I have doubled it."

"Good work," his master said. "You are a good and faithful servant. You have been faithful over this small amount, so now I will give you much more."

Then the man with the $1,000 came and said, "Sir, I knew you were a hard man, and I was afraid you would rob me of what I earned, so I hid your money in the earth and here it is!"

But his master replied, "Wicked man! Lazy slave! Since you knew I would demand your profit, you should at least have put my money into the bank so I could have some interest. Take the money from this man and give it to the man with the $10,000. For the man who uses well what he is given shall be given more, and he shall have abundance. But from the man who is unfaithful, even what little responsibility he has shall be taken from him."

– Bible, Matthew 25:14-30

PROVERBS AND MAXIMS

Whenever you are to do a thing, though it can never be known but to yourself, ask yourself how you would act were all the world looking at you, and act accordingly.

— *Thomas Jefferson*

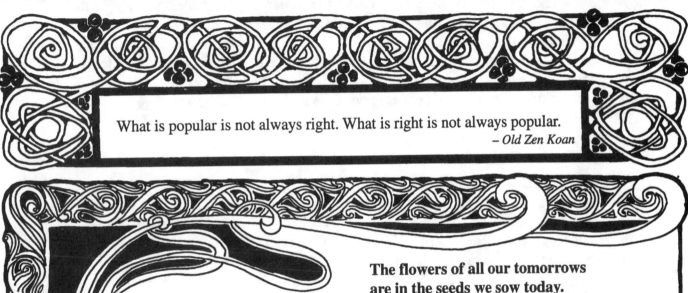

What is popular is not always right. What is right is not always popular.

— *Old Zen Koan*

**The flowers of all our tomorrows
are in the seeds we sow today.**

— *Cicero*

**Before enlightenment I carried logs of wood and pails of water.
After enlightenment I carried logs of wood and pails of water.**

— *Old Zen Koan*

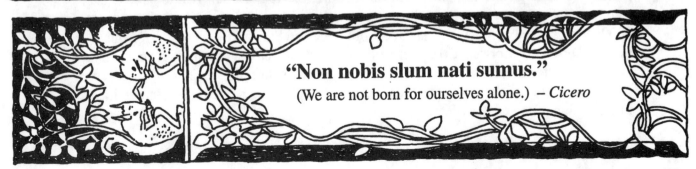

"Non nobis slum nati sumus."
(We are not born for ourselves alone.) — *Cicero*

HEROES AND HEROINES

EDDIE AIKAU (1946–1978)

Born in Kahului, Maui, Eddie is probably best known as a big wave surfer, but his strength of character and his willingness to sacrifice for others will be his enduring tribute. As a lifeguard, he risked his life to save over a thousand people during a nine year period. As a member of the 1978 Hokulea crew, he gave his life in an heroic attempt to rescue the crew. Eddie was fearless in surfing the big waves of Waimea; regularly challenging waves over 20 feet, and on November 19, 1967 he caught a 35 foot monster at Waimea Bay. Whether he was surfing, lifeguarding, playing music or being with his family, his life had an unique focus and intensity. Before anyone had to ask for a volunteer to paddle for land when the Hokulea capsized, Eddie was untying the surfboard. "Eddie would go."

NELLIE BLY (1867–1922)

Born as Elizabeth Cochrane in a small town in Pennsylvania, a small girl with older brothers, she quickly learned how to survive with bravery and daring. She and her mother moved to Pittsburgh after her father died. Nellie decided she wanted to be a writer. She responded to a newspaper editorial critical of women's rights, won the respect of the editor and was hired as a reporter. Unable to use her name, she chose a name from a popular Stephen Foster song, Nellie Bly. She became well-known for her first-hand accounts of social inequity. She went into the slums, factories, hospitals, orphanages and prisons, exposing the terrible conditions. In New York City, working on the staff of the "World" for Joseph Pulitzer, she wrote such a devastating article about Blackwell's Island, the city's mental hospital, that it caused immediate reform and improvements.

THOMAS JEFFERSON (1743–1826)

Born at Shadwell, a tobacco plantation in Virginia, Thomas Jefferson was a member of one of Virginia's most distinguished families. He studied to become a lawyer, but practiced only a few years before entering politics. He became active in efforts to separate the colonies from English domination, and when he was elected as a delegate to the Second Continental Congress, he became the primary author of the Declaration of Independence. In 1800, he was elected as the third president of the United States. His accomplishments included efforts to reorganize the courts of law, to establish a system of public education, and to guarantee religious freedom. His skills in business, farming, inventory, language, architecture, education, government, and community planning made him an integral leader in the design of the United States.

ELEANOR ROOSEVELT (1884–1962)

Born in New York City, her father was Elliott Roosevelt, the younger brother of Theodore Roosevelt. Eleanor led a very troubled childhood; both her parents died while she was young (her father was an alcoholic and her mother was neurotic, preoccupied with social life and embarrassed at Eleanor's homeliness), and she went to live with her maternal grandmother. Convinced she would never marry, Eleanor plunged into social work. In 1905 she married her cousin, Franklin Delano Roosevelt. As a president's wife, she was quite independent and continued her interests in social service and modeled civic and national responsibility. After her husband's death, she served on the United Nations Commission on Human Rights and was instrumental in the completion of the Universal Declaration of Human Rights, which was adopted by the United Nations in 1948. She also worked with President Kennedy as an advisor for the Peace Corps and chair of the President's Commission on the Status of Women.

HARRY S. TRUMAN (1884–1972)

Born on a farm in Lamar, Missouri, he started as a farmer, but following service in the army during World War I, Harry became a partner in a men's clothing store. When the business failed, he turned to politics and became a county commissioner. In 1934, he was elected to the Senate and earned a reputation as a person of integrity as a special investigator of the national defense program. Supported by the conservatives, he replaced Wallace as Vice President and became President when FDR died in 1945. His first responsibility was to preside over the end of World War II as he authorized the dropping of the first atomic bomb on Hiroshima, Japan. His tough decisions guided America through some difficult years. Never shirking his duties and always accepting full responsibility for his decisions, he had a sign on his desk that read, "The buck stops here."

BOOKER T. WASHINGTON (1856–1915)

Born in Franklin County, Virginia as Booker Taliaferro (The Washington was later added) and a slave, he and his family were liberated by the Union Army in 1865. In return for being allowed a few hours of school each afternoon, his stepfather forced him to work in a salt mine in the morning and evenings. At age 16, he left home for Hampton Institute, proved himself to be an excellent student with scrupulous work habits and graduated in 1876. He taught in a rural school for two years and joined the faculty at Hampton Institute where he supervised 100 Native Americans who had been admitted. In 1881, he was appointed to the task of founding Tuskegee Institute, a school for blacks. Under his leadership it became an important force in black education and he served as president until his death in 1915. In 1895, Washington gave his famous "Atlanta Compromise" speech where he renounced agitation and protest in favor of improving job skills and usefulness. Outwardly conciliatory, Washington secretly financed and encouraged attempts and lawsuits to block southern movers to disfranchise and segregate blacks.

PUT RESPONSIBILITY INTO ACTION

- Clean up your area after lunch and encourage your friends to do the same.
- Follow through on all assignments at school and chores at home.
- Do your chores at home without being asked.
- Look for something extra to do at home or in your community.
- Organize a beach or public park clean-up.
- Keep a promise.
- Express your anger with appropriate words and actions.
- Follow through on commitments to organizations that you join; clubs, sports teams, committees.
- Do some volunteer work in the community.

COMMUNITY SERVICE IDEAS

- Clean up your "own back yard" by collecting rubbish and recycling items around the school and home.
- Organize a graffiti clean-up party.
- Volunteer at a local Community Center helping elementary students with recreation, crafts, and other activities.
- Sponsor a canned food drive at your school. Take the food to a local soup kitchen and help feed the needy.
- Make informational posters encouraging members of your community to recycle. Provide the address and phone number of recycling services available in your area.
- Find an open area on your school grounds and plant a tree.
- Read your local paper and find a family or individual in need. (i.e. Victims of natural disasters, house fires, robbery, etc.) Provide them with food, clothing, or a collection of money from students in your school.

BOOKS ON RESPONSIBILITY

Horton Hatches the Egg. Dr. Seuss. New York: Simon Schuster, 1940.

The Book of Virtues. William J. Bennett, ed. New York: Simon and Schuster, 1993.
  "Aristotle on Self-Discipline" – p. 101
  "Boy Wanted" – p. 78
  "The Bridge Builder" – p. 223
  "The Declaration of Independence" – p. 251
  "Etiquette in a Nutshell" – p. 201
  "Federalist No. 55" – p. 263
  "George Washington's Rules of Civility" – p. 74
  "The Golden Touch" – p. 68
  "Icarus and Daedalus" – p. 211
  "If You Were" – p. 207
  "Men Without Chests" – p. 263
  "The Sword of Damocles" – p. 213

Compassion

SUPPORTIVE VALUES

Service • Generosity

DEFINITIONS

The desire to ease others' suffering.

Compassion is a sympathetic awareness of another's distress combined with a desire to alleviate it. Even stronger than the word *sympathetic* is the word *empathetic,* which requires us to walk in another's shoes, truly striving to understand the plight of the less fortunate and seek ways to help. The words of the 14th Dalai Lama expand on this definition: ". . . each of us has responsibility for all humankind. It is time for us to think of other people as true brothers and sisters and to be concerned with their welfare, with lessening their suffering . . . we should think more about the future and benefit of all humanity."

Service and **Generosity** are ways in which we can demonstrate our compassion for others. Service is a contribution of time for the benefit of others. Generosity suggests giving freely and liberally of that which we have without expecting anything in return. Kahlil Gibran writes of the difference between service and generosity, "You give but little when you give of your possessions. It is when you give of yourself that you truly give."

PURPOSE

Students often recognize the plight of the homeless and hungry in their city and in the world. Amazingly, these are the same students who can be so callous toward each other and from whom critical remarks and cruel actions toward those with differences abound. Recalling our first month's emphasis on respect, along with partner values of acceptance and kindness, we can see how compassion connects. By putting the values of compassion and acceptance into action we can enable our students to help the child who is having a difficult time making friends and be of service by offering friendship. We can seek ways in which we can be of service in our classes: by volunteering to help, in our homes; by being helpful beyond our chores, in our schools; by doing litter clean-ups, taking care of our areas of play and study, in our communities; by contributing to needy causes, in our state, country, and world; by being aware of those less fortunate and finding ways to assist those outside of our personal world.

Compassion

Day One:
Consider the dictionary definition of compassion and then write a definition in your own words.

Day Two:
Write your own definition of compassion on a strip of construction paper or poster board to be cut out and decorated for a bookmark. Use the bookmark as a constant reminder of the need for compassion in daily life.

Day Three:
One simple definition that has been given for compassion is "the desire to ease others' suffering." Brainstorm about lives of people you know whose actions represent a burning desire to "ease the suffering" of troubled people. Select one person for a "compassionate person" award.

Day Four:
With a partner, read and pronounce as best you can the word compassion in other languages (page 51). Research the cultures represented to find out ways compassion is demonstrated in each.

Day Five:
Rewrite a biography of a famous person whose actions demonstrated compassion in a way that made a difference in the lives of others. Add the rewritten biography to a class anthology to be presented to an adult literacy class or an English as a second language class.

Day Six:
Make a list of ways boys and girls of your age can show compassion for home bound elderly persons in your community.

Day Seven:
A Native American saying admonished us to "walk a mile in the shoes of another before judging that person." Explain how this saying applies to human compassion for one's fellow human beings.

Day Eight:
Brainstorm as many words as you can that have meanings similar to compassion. Kind hearted and generous are two to get you started! Use a thesaurus to help you.

Day Nine:
Start a brand new brainstorming session to generate a list of word "opposites" for compassionate. Selfish and unresponsive are two for starters.

Day Ten:
Use your word lists from the past two days to create a word find or crossword puzzle.

Day Eleven:
As you worked with the word lists, what kinds of feelings did the negative and positive words from the two lists create? Can you think of actions directed toward you in the past that make you identify with some of the words? How about your own actions toward others?

Day Twelve:
Plan a campaign for your class to initiate a program to demonstrate compassion for physically or mentally handicapped students of your own age.

Day Thirteen:
Name some ways that teachers and administrators in your school demonstrate compassion for students and their families as needs emerge.

Day Fourteen:
Take a very private look at yourself to determine if your friends, family, and acquaintances would consider you a truly compassionate person. Ponder your conclusions honestly and think of behavior modifications if you feel they are in order.

Day Fifteen:
Select a hero or heroine to research (page 60-61) and determine the influence of their compassion for others in a time beyond their own life.

Day Sixteen:
Mother Teresa was often criticized for her ministry to the world's poorest and most downtrodden people by skeptics who felt her work was wasted because the beneficiaries were hopeless. What is your opinion?

Day Seventeen:
Survey your classmates to determine their feelings about the level of compassion shown in your community for underprivileged children. Graph your findings.

Day Eighteen:
Draft a letter to a community leader to promote social activism of some nature based on the findings of your survey. Send the survey results along with the letter.

Day Nineteen:
Make a list of ways you have shown compassion in a way that has made a difference in the lives or feelings of family members or friends in the past week. Ponder your list. Is it as long as you would like for it to be?

Day Twenty:
Reflect on the meaning and implications for the future of embracing compassion for others as a life shaping value.

COMPASSION IN OTHER LANGUAGES

Chinese   *ren*   perfect virtue; free from selfishness; the ideal of Confucius (the inner love for men which prompts to just deeds); benevolence; charity; humility

French   *la compassion*   pity, the feelings inspired by the misfortune of others

German   *mitgefhl*   compassion, sympathy

Hawaiian   *lokomaika'i*   kind, humane, gracious, benevolent

oko – within, inside
maika'i – goodness, righteousness

Japanese   *jin*   an important word mentioned by Confucius

Korean   *yun min*   commiseration

Latin   *misericodia*   suffering together with another
cum – together with
pati – to suffer

Spanish   *compasión*   compassion, pity, sympathy

Tagalog   *pakikiramay*   to feel sympathy and act in charity on behalf of someone in need

DISCUSSION QUESTIONS

• Why should we be compassionate toward others?

• For whom should we feel compassionate?

• How can we show compassion for someone?

• What are some of the events around the world that make you sad? What causes this feeling of sadness?

• What are some things we can do which help us deal with this kind of sadness?

• Is there anything we can do to help the people caught up in the events which cause human suffering? What can we do if there is not a specific way to help them directly?

• Have you ever volunteered to work on a service project? What kind of work did you do? Who and how did it help? How did it make you feel to volunteer?

• Have you ever given any of your personal belongings to someone?

• Have you ever contributed money you have earned yourself?

• What people in our lives are in need of compassion? Why? What are the feelings you have about these people? Do your feelings ever inspire you to do something?

• Are you ever in need of compassion? Who helps you? How quickly can you identify this need in someone else?

• Is it easy or difficult for you to do something to help someone in need? Why?

• Is it easier to give money to an organization than to work as a volunteer? Why? Is one form of help more important than another?

• Who is your neighbor—the person next door, the one down the street, the one across town?

• Is our concept of neighbor expanding? Is our responsibility expanding?

• Do you think people are becoming *more* or *less* concerned about the suffering in our world? Why?

STORIES AND THOUGHTS FROM SPIRITUAL TRADITIONS

Hinduism

The true "Hindu" is that person who, on seeing violence perpetrated against any living thing ("hinsa"), experiences the suffering ("dukha") as if it was his own.

– Tradition

When there is attachment to desires, there is pain.
Renunciation of attachments will lead to non-attachment.
Non-attachment will lead to love.
Love will lead to compassion.

– Tradition

Rare are those who appreciate the merits of others.
Rare are those who hold the poor in affection.
Rare are those who remain calm in the battle, and
Rare are those who are distressed at the grief of others.

– Tradition

Buddhism

Compassion is the wish to relieve the sufferings of living beings. Boundless compassion is the wish to relieve the sufferings of infinite living beings without exception.

Zen Buddhism

It isn't only upon the cultivation of such love and desire for universal salvation that all human beings will be equally able to share in the benefits of science and technology in the great, harmonious unity of this one world.

Christianity

"Be compassionate as your God is compassionate."   *– Bible, Luke 6:36*

"When Jesus saw the crowds, he had compassion for them,
  because they were harassed and helpless, like sheep
  without a shepherd."   *– Bible, Matthew 9:36*

"Put on then, as God's chosen people, compassion,
kindness, lowliness, meekness and patience."   *– Bible, Colossians 3:12*

The Parable of the Good Samaritan

One day an expert on Moses' laws came to test Jesus' orthodoxy by asking him this question: "Teacher, what does a man need to do to live forever in heaven?"

Jesus replied, "What does Moses' law say about it?"

"It says," he replied, "that you must love the Lord your God with all your heart, and with all your soul, and with all your strength, and with all your mind. And you must love your neighbor just as much as you love yourself."

"Right!" Jesus told him. "Do this and you shall live!"

The man wanted to justify his lack of love for some kinds of people, so he asked, "Which neighbors?"

Jesus replied with an illustration: "A Jew going on a trip from Jerusalem to Jericho was attacked by bandits. They stripped him of his clothes and money and beat him up and left him lying half dead beside the road.

By chance a Jewish priest came along; and when he saw the man lying there, he crossed to the other side of the road and passed him by. A Jewish Temple assistant walked over and looked at him lying there, but then went on.

But a despised Samaritan came along, and when he saw him, he felt deep pity. Kneeling beside him the Samaritan soothed his wounds with medicine and bandaged them. Then he put the man on his donkey and walked along beside him till they came to an inn, where he nursed him through the night. The next day he handed the innkeeper two twenty dollar bills and told him to take care of the man. 'If his bill runs higher than that,' he said, 'I'll pay the difference the next time I am here.'

Now which of these three would you say was a neighbor to the bandits' victim?"

The man replied, "The one who showed him some pity."

"Yes," Jesus said, "now go and do the same."   *– Bible, Luke 10: 25-37*

Casting the First Stone

Jesus was at the Temple. A crowd soon gathered, and he sat down and talked to them. As he was speaking, the Jewish leaders and Pharisees brought a woman caught in adultery and placed her out in front of the staring crowd.

"Teacher," they said to Jesus, "this woman was caught in the very act of adultery. Moses' law says to kill her. What about it?"

They were trying to trap him into saying something they could use against him, but Jesus stooped down and wrote in the dust with his finger. They kept demanding an answer, so he stood up again and said, "All right, hurl the stones at her until she dies. But only he who never sinned may throw the first!"

Then he stooped down again and wrote some more in the dust. And the Jewish leaders slipped away one by one, beginning with the eldest, until only Jesus was left in front of the crowd with the woman.

Then Jesus stood up again and said to her, "Where are your accusers? Didn't even one of them condemn you?"

"No, sir," she said.

And Jesus said, "Neither do I. Go and sin no more."   *– Bible, John 8:1-11*

Islam

The Messenger of Allah said: 'O Women of the Faithful, do not think it is a little thing which you give to your neighbor even if it is a small part of the leg of a goat.' (Abu Dawud included the addition:) 'Give gifts to each other for surely gifts take away ill feeling from the heart.'

321: Hadith
Bukhari: Book of Good Manners
– The Essential Teachings of Islam p. 207

The people of the Prophet's house killed a goat. Then they gave way portions to the poor, so that there remained only a portion thereof. The Prophet asked, 'What remains thereof?' They said, 'Nothing but the shoulder.' The Prophet said, 'Nay, all of it remains except its shoulder, for the reward thereof is eternal.'

– Selections from Mishkat-ul-masabi [110] p. 29

Chinese

"In the service of one's prince, repeated scolding can only lead to
a loss of favor; in friendship, it can only lead to estrangement."　　*– Confucius*

"Goodness cannot be obtained till what is difficult has been duly
done. He who has done this may be called Good."　　*– Confucius*

"In his dealings with individuals and with society, let him move
without loss of result. In the management of his breath, let him be
like the mother bird, brooding like the Spirit, quiet, without effort."　*– Lao Tzu*

"To balance our earthly nature and to cultivate our heavenly nature,
tread the Middle Path."　　*– Lao Tzu*

Once when Yen Hui and Tzu-lu were waiting upon him the Master said, "Suppose each of you were to tell his wish." Tzu-lu said, "I should like to have carriages and horses, clothes and fur rugs, share them with my friends and feel no annoyance if they were returned to me the worse for wear." Yen Hui said, "I should never like to boast of my good qualities nor make a fuss about the trouble I take on behalf of others." Tzu-lu said, "A thing I would like is to hear the Master's wish." The Master said, "In dealing with the aged, to be of comfort to them; in dealing with friends, to be of good faith with them; in dealing with the young, to cherish them."

– The Analects, Book V

　　　　　　Character Education Year 1 Grades 6–12　　**55**

Act without lust of result; work without anxiety, taste without attachment to flavor; esteem small things great and few things many; repel violence with gentleness. Do great things while they are yet small, hard things while they are yet easy; for all things, how great or hard so ever, have a beginning when they are little and easy. The wise man considers even easy things hard, so that even hard things are easy to him.

— Tao Te Ching

The oceans and the rivers attract the streams by their skill in being lower than they; thus they are the masters thereof. So the Wise Man, to be above men, speaks lowly; and to precede them acts with humility.

So then do all men delight to honor him, and grow not weary of him. He contends not against any man; therefore no man is able to contend against him.

— Tao Te Ching

Judaism

If Not Higher

There was a newcomer who arrived in a village and was becoming acquainted with the people. The villagers were telling him about the rabbi who lived in their village who, every Friday, ascended to heaven. The newcomer was understandably skeptical. He found out where the rabbi lived and hid behind a tree near his house one Friday morning to watch him. He saw the rabbi leave his house on a wintry morning, chop down a tree and cut up the wood. Then he followed him to the house of an elderly woman who lived just outside the village, quietly leave the wood outside her house, then return home. The newcomer decided to stay and live in the village and ever after, when he would hear the villagers talk about their rabbi who ascended to heaven every Friday, he would reply, "if not higher."

Hebrew Brothers

Once, long ago there lived a farmer named Seth who lived in the land of Israel. He had two sons, named Dan and Joel. When they were young, they followed Seth all about as he farmed the land, learning their tasks well. Every spring and every fall, they helped Seth plant the seeds. Then they would watch as the wheat grew and grew until it was over their heads.

When the wheat was finally ripe, Seth would harvest it with his sickle and the two brothers would help him to tie up the bushels, load them onto their donkey, and take them to be threshed. For many years, the boys and their father worked happily side by side. The boys grew taller and stronger as Seth grew older and tired from his labors. Finally, one day, Seth said to his sons, "You are not only good men and good farmers, but you have been very good sons. I am growing old and it is difficult for me to plow and plant. I no longer have the strength to harvest and thresh the wheat that we grow. I am weak and so very tired. My dear sons, I feel that soon I will die."

The two brothers were greatly saddened by their father's words, but listened as he continued. "I will divide my land in half so that when I am gone Dan will have one part, and Joel the other. I trust that you will always be as good to one another as you have been to me. I know that you shall always be friends and take good care of one another."

Soon after that, their dear father died. The land was divided in half and each of the brothers built a house on their part. Joel married a wonderful woman named Miriam. They were happy and over time, had three sons. As his family grew, Joel added rooms to their house, and his sons helped with all the work just as Joel and Dan had helped their father.

Dan, on the other hand, did not mary. He lived alone in a small house on his half of the land. He was happy to visit Joel and his family whenever he could.

One year, the rains did not fall as expected. The crops were poor and the harvest was very small. Neither Joel nor Dan had many bushels to thresh. One night, Joel was distressed and could not sleep. "What's the matter?" asked Miriam.

Joel sat up. "I am thinking about my poor brother," he said. "I am worried for he is all alone. We have our sons to help us and care for us when we are old. Dan is alone and has no one. He has so much less than we do. It is not fair that we should have the same amount of land and the same amount of wheat."

Miriam looked at him thoughtfully. "What will you do?"

Joel sat quietly for a moment then said, "I must take some of our wheat to my brother." So he dressed quickly and went out into the night. He loaded up his sleepy donkey with as much wheat as it could carry and set off for his brother's house. Once there, he silently placed all the wheat on his brother's threshing floor and returned home.

The very same night, Dan was also sleepless. He paced back and forth, thinking about his brother, Joel. "My dear brother has a wife and three sons to feed and care for. I have no one to care for but myself. It is not fair that we should have the same amount of land and the same amount of wheat. I must take some of my wheat to my brother!" he thought. So he went out into the night, loaded his donkey with wheat and took it to his brother's house. Silently, he unloaded the wheat and left it on his brother's threshing floor.

The next morning, when Joel saw all the wheat that there was on his threshing floor he was puzzled. "Why, there doesn't seem to be any less than there was yesterday. I must take some more to Dan tonight."

Dan was also surprised when he saw all the wheat on his threshing floor. "I must not have taken very much to my brother's house. I will be sure to take much more tonight."

That night, once again, Joel took wheat to Dan's house and Dan brought wheat to Joel's house. The next day, each brother had just as much wheat as the day before. Joel was very perplexed and spoke to his family about it. "Perhaps you need help," Miriam said. "Yes, tonight we will all help you," added the boys.

So that night Joel, Miriam and their sons loaded up the donkey with wheat and each carried as much as he could to Dan's house.

At the same time, Dan was starting out with a great load of wheat on his donkey and as much as he could carry in his arms to take to Joel.

The two brothers happened to meet halfway at the very spot which divided their father's property in half. As soon as they saw each other, they understood what had been happening. They did not need to speak to understand the concern that each had for the other. They dropped their bundles of wheat and embraced each other warmly.

Then, ever so sweetly, a voice swept around them singing, "How good it is for brothers to live in friendship."

Hundreds of years after that meeting, a city called Jerusalem had grown where Seth's farm had once been. In that city, a great king named Solomon had a temple built on the spot where the brothers met and embraced that night long ago. And there, at the temple, the same sweet voice has been heard to sing, "How good it is for brothers to live in friendship."

PROVERBS AND MAXIMS

You give but little when you give of your possessions.
It is when you give of yourself that you truly give. *– Kahlil Gibran*

The worst sin toward our fellow creatures is not to hate them,
but to be indifferent to them; that's the essence of inhumanity.
– George Bernard Shaw

Life is like a tennis game.
You can't win without serving.
– Arthur Ashe

The test of our progress is not whether we add more to the
abundance of those who have much; it is whether we
provide enough for those who have too little.
– Franklin D. Roosevelt

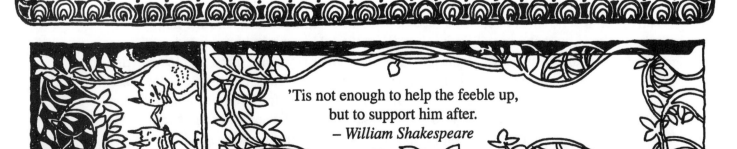

'Tis not enough to help the feeble up,
but to support him after.
– William Shakespeare

Character Education Year 1 Grades 6–12   **59**

HEROES AND HEROINES

JANE ADDAMS (1860–1935)

Born in Cedarville, Illinois, she was the youngest of five children. Her mother died, when Jane was still a baby, and she was taken care of by her sisters and brother. She became aware of poverty at age seven when she saw some poor children and she immediately announced that she wanted to build a house where they could come and play. After college, during a trip to Europe, she discovered a way to help the poor by living among them. She searched the slums of Chicago until she found a mansion in disrepair. She and a friend, Ellen Stan, fixed it up, moved in, and cared for the children of working mothers; thus Hull House was founded. In addition, she fought for child labor laws, safe working conditions, adult education, day nurseries, better housing and women's suffrage. She was awarded the Nobel Peace Prize in 1931.

PEARL SYDENSTRICKER BUCK (1892–1973)

Born in Hillsboro, West Virginia, while her parents were on a furlough from their mission field in China, she spent most of her first forty years in China, returning to the United States only for college and graduate studies. She married John Lossing Buck in 1917 and they lived in Nanking, China from 1921–34. She developed a deep compassion for the Chinese people and expressed this concern in many of her 85 novels, short stories and books of non-fiction. She was awarded the Nobel Prize for Literature in 1938, mostly because of her novel "The Good Earth" (1931), which also won her a Pulitzer Prize. She continued to promote social tolerance, was active in child welfare work (especially for disadvantaged Asian children) and founded Welcome House, an adoption agency for Asian-American children.

FATHER DAMIEN (1840–1889)

Born as Joseph de Veuster in Tremeloo, Belgium, he followed his brother to a contemplative monastery where he experienced a vision of St. Francis Xavier and was convinced that he should become a missionary. He substituted for his brother in a missionary party that was sailing for Hawai'i in 1863. Upon arrival he was ordained a priest, to be known as Father Damien, and began regular work as a priest in a local parish. When he heard about the conditions of those suffering from Hansen's disease on Molokai, he decided they needed a resident priest. His ministry was a life of compassion, Christian humanism and service to people who had been separated and discarded from society. He served in Kalaupapa from 1873 until Hansen's disease claimed his life in 1889.

SWAMI VIVEKANANDA (1863–1902)

Born in India, he became India's first spiritual and cultural ambassador to the West. He presented a message to the World Parliament of Religions, held in Chicago in 1893, that focused on the unity of humankind and the harmony of religions. He wanted to create a bridge between the East and West by exchanging the message of India's ancient spirituality with scientific and industrial ideas of the West. He founded the Ramakrishna Order of India which is widely known for its charity; running hospitals and schools, rebuilding rural India and emergency relief work. He regarded the service of all people as the highest form of worship. He continued to teach the underlying truth of all religions, and the government of India declared his birthday a national holiday.

DALAI LAMA (1935–)

Born in the village of Takster, Tibet, he was known by the name of Lhamo. Following the death of the thirteenth Dalai Lama in 1933, and through a combination of prayer, tradition, and visions, monks were led to the home of a peasant family. There they were greeted by a two-year old boy, who immediately crawled into the lap of one of the monks and touched a rosary that had belonged to the Dalai Lama. After a series of tests, the boy was taken to Lhasa, the capital of Tibet, and formally installed as the Dalai Lama at age four. When the Chinese invaded Tibet in 1950, the Dalai Lama's life was in danger; he was forced to leave in 1959 and has been in exile since then. In spite of the atrocities committed by the Chinese on the Tibetan people, he has continued to speak of forgiveness, justice, and living together in harmony. When asked about his religion, Tibetan Buddhism, he replied, "My religion is kindness." He was awarded the Nobel Peace Prize in 1989.

MOTHER TERESA (1910–1997)

Born in Skopje, Yugoslavia, as Agnes Gonxha Bojaxhiu, she was the youngest of three children born to an Albanian couple. Her mother was a devout Catholic and took her young daughter with her on visits to the sick and the needy. After prayerful consideration, Agnes decided "to go out and give the life of Christ to the people;" she was twelve years old. She joined the sisters of Loreto and left for Calcutta in 1929. She taught high school until 1948, learning both Bengali and Hindi during this time. Agnes took her first vows of poverty, chastity and obedience in 1931, selected Teresa as her name and took her final vows in 1937. In 1946 she received a call to help the poor and formed the Missionaries of Charity in 1950. She added a fourth vow to the traditional three; "to give wholehearted, free service to the very poorest." Her work in the slums of Calcutta led to the awarding of the Nobel Peace Prize in 1979. She possessed a serene spirituality, a sense of joyful compassion, and a reverence for human life. She wrote, "We can do no great things, only small things with great love."

PUT COMPASSION INTO ACTION

- Be friendly to someone who needs a friend.
- Do helpful things at home without being asked.
- Be generous with your time and your belongings.
- Create and participate in a litter control program at your school.
- Pick up litter, wherever you are, instead of walking past it.
- Plan and participate in a canned food collection for a local charity.
- Look for ways to help in any situation without being asked.
- Put someone else's needs before your own.
- Look for ways to help someone in the community.
- Try to understand why a family member or friend is sad.
- Forgive someone who has hurt you.
- Talk with your family about the problems of the homeless. Find a way to help.
- Try to understand someone you disagree with or don't like.

COMMUNITY SERVICE IDEAS

- Recycle aluminum cans. Put the money earned into a local food bank.
- Collect food for a local food bank.
- Offer to help an elderly neighbor with their yard work; get a friend to help you.
- Take a meal to someone who is ill.
- Volunteer with the Red Cross or another similar organization.
- Volunteer at a local hospital or senior center. Help the elderly with shopping, errands, or chores.
- Replace the signs about responsibility that you hung last month in your town with new signs reminding everyone to be compassionate toward each other.
- Write a letter of compassion to a victim of some recent tragedy. If this person has suffered a serious material loss, collect some of the lost items and send along with your letter (for example, flood victims might need clothes, shoes, a radio, etc.).
- Create a school bulletin board where students and teachers can recognize people within the school who have demonstrated great compassion.
- Choose a historical figure who represents compassion. Write your own or find in the library a short play which tells about this person's compassionate acts. Perform the play for your community. Donate the proceeds to a local shelter for the homeless or other charity which you feel demonstrates compassion in its everyday work.

BOOKS ON COMPASSION

Alexander and the Terrible, Horrible, Very Bad, Mixed-Up Day. Judith Viorst. New York: Atheneum, 1972.

All I See. Cynthia Rylant. New York: Orchard Books, 1988.

Fly Away Home. Eve Bunting. New York. Clarion Books, 1991.

The Giving Tree. Shel Silverstein. New York: Harper & Row, 1964.

A Japanese Fairytale. Jane Ike. New YOrk: F. Warne, 1982.

Shoebag. Mary Jones. New York: Scholastic, 1990.

Zoo. Anthony Brown. New York: KNopf, 1992.

The Book of Virtues. William J. Bennett, ed. New York: Simon and Schuster, 1993.
  "Count That Day Lost" – p. 171

A Call to Character. Colin Greer and Herbert Kohl, eds. New York: Harper Collins Publishers, 1995.
  "In Memory of Our Cat, Ralph" – p. 330
  "A Raisin in the Sun" – p. 320
  "What I Have Lived For" – p. 364

The Moral Compass. William J. Bennett, ed. New York: Simon and Schuster, 1995.
  "Abraham and the Old Man" – p. 735
  "I Sought My Soul" – p. 744
  "The Legend Beautiful" – p. 735
  "The Student" – p. 784
  "True Saintliness" – p. 737

December
Faith

SUPPORTIVE
VALUES

Hope • Trust

DEFINITIONS

Belief in and loyalty to a god, person, idea or something which cannot be proven.

Faith is having complete allegiance to a person or an idea. It refers to a belief in God and belief in something for which there is no proof. Faith speaks of confidence and conviction; qualities of inner strength. In this way, faith refers to belief in oneself and the quality of fidelity to one's promises.

Hope is to cherish a desire with every expectation that it will be fulfilled; to long for something with the same expectation. It also refers to someone or something on which this expectation is centered.

Trust is the assured reliance on the character, ability, strength, or truth of someone or something. It refers to the placing of confidence, dependence, reliance, or hope in someone or something.

PURPOSE

Most lists of universal/democratic values would not include faith. However, we have both an opportunity and obligation to include faith as one of the primary values. Now that we have established respect and responsibility as the two "umbrella" values and have added compassion as an emphasis of including others, we add faith as the value that will lead our students toward the transcendent qualities of life. Thus, we move from self to others and, then, to that which is beyond (and within) our human experience. As Americans, we draw primarily from the rich Jewish and Christian traditions. As people and citizens of a global community, we want students to learn from the wisdom of different cultures and other world faiths. We must learn to live with and embrace diversity.

Faith

Day One:
Discuss the definition of faith as explained on page 65.

Day Two:
Write a personal definition of faith that makes sense to you in your own words. Make a bookmark out of it and use it daily.

Day Three:
Use the well-known proverb that describes faith as "a bird that sings when the dawn is still dark" as a starter for a journal entry about an event in your own life that required you to rely on a personal faith.

Day Four:
Think of a person of your acquaintance who demonstrates a strong faith that sets a good example for other people. Describe the person's personality.

Day Five:
Explore understandings of ways parents show faith in the future by encouraging their children's dreams and goals.

Day Six:
Name three things siblings can do to create open communication between each other in order to share a common faith in a set of core values.

Day Seven:
How do students' personal career goals reflect their faith in themselves?

Day Eight:
Tell why it is important to have faith in the money we use. What would happen if this faith did not exist?

Day Nine:
Do you have faith in yourself to 1) do your homework correctly 2) recognize a dangerous situation 3) say no to drugs/alcohol/violence 4) be a good son or daughter 5) succeed in life?

Day Ten:
Brainstorm, research, and illustrate symbols of faith.

Day Eleven:
Is faith an easy value to embrace? Are there risks? Are there benefits?

Day Twelve:
Agree or disagree with and discuss the implications of the statement, "A person's beliefs are from the head, but faith is from the heart."

Day Thirteen:
Find a song whose central theme is faith. Ponder the words of the song and research its history. Discuss instances in which music through the ages has helped to strengthen, sustain or renew faith.

Day Fourteen:
Use the yellow pages of your local phone directory (or other appropriate source) to tabulate the number of religious institutions in your community. Try to determine the number of different religious faiths represented. Are there more or fewer than you would have thought?

Day Fifteen:
Read the Declaration of Independence of the United States of America and discuss the ways in which it testifies to the strong faith its signers held in the promise of the future for a democratic society.

Day Sixteen:
Act out a scene from world history to portray an act of courage or self-sacrifice on the part of a character demonstrating a strong faith in a specific cause. Research the setting and the period carefully in order to accurately portray the event.

Day Seventeen:
Read a story on the life of Martin Luther King to find out how his famous "I have a dream" speech reflected his faith in the future. Read a story about faith from pages 69-78.

Day Eighteen:
Predict what a world without faith would be like. How would people behave? Would the world be a better or worse place? How would your community be different? Write a short story with a setting in this faithless world.

Day Nineteen:
In small groups, research a major religious faith not practiced by anyone in your class. Present to the total class a report on the main premise of that religion and the ways in which followers demonstrate their faith. At the end of all the reports, decide if there are similarities in the beliefs.

Day Twenty:
Reflect on the implications of what embracing faith as a lifelong value means to you personally.

FAITH IN OTHER LANGUAGES

Chinese	*qian* *cheng*	to act with reverence; devout; sincere sincere; true; honest
French	*la foi*	faithfulness in fulfilling one's commitments, loyalty; confidence in something or someone; believing in God or a body of religious truths
German	*glaube*	faith, belief, credence, trust, religious faith, creed
Hawaiian	*mana'o'i'o*	"faith, confidence" (mana'o means "thought, idea, belief, opinion" and 'i'o means "true, genuine, significant, real")
Japanese	*seijitsu*	make things you said happen and the house will be full of the treasure sei—make things you said happen jitsu—to fill up the house full of treasure
Korean	*shin nyum*	belief with confidence
Latin	*fides*	trust
Spanish	*fe*	faith, trust
Tagalog	*pananalig*	to trust and believe in God or an idea without proof

DISCUSSION QUESTIONS

- What areas of your life are helped or strengthened by faith? Relationships? Homework?

- What are the obstacles to a strong faith in a god? Too busy, don't understand?

- When do people need faith? Sickness, personal challenge?

- What or who else do you have faith in? Why?

- What does your religious faith have in common with other faiths?

- What are the areas of life in which people have faith? Are they all equally important?

- What are the causes of doubt and disbelief? Is doubt ever helpful? Can life be complete or happy without faith in something or someone beyond yourself?

- What aspects of religious faith are especially helpful? What would you change?

- Is faith helpful in solving problems and meeting life's challenges?

- What do we have in common with other world faiths? Can one faith be right for everybody?

STORIES AND THOUGHTS FROM SPIRITUAL TRADITIONS

Hinduism

Among those who are purified by their good deeds, there are four kinds of men who worship me: the world-weary, the seeker for knowledge, the seeker for happiness and the man of spiritual discrimination. The man of discrimination is the highest of these. He is continually united with me. He devotes himself to me always, and to no other. For I am very dear to the man, and he is dear to me.

> Certainly, all these are noble: But the man of discrimination
> I see as my very Self.
> For he alone loves me
> Because I am myself: The last and only goal
> Of his devoted heart.
> Through many a long life
> His discrimination ripens: He makes me his refuge,
> Knows that Brahman is all.
> How rare are such great ones!

Men whose discrimination has been blunted by worldly desires, establish this or that ritual or cult and resort to various deities, according to the impulse of their inborn natures. But it does not matter what deity a devotee chooses to worship. If he has faith, I make his faith unwavering. Endowed with the faith I give him, he worships that deity, and gets from it everything he prays for. In reality, I alone am the giver.

– Bhagavad Gita

For he who turns to God his face, lifetimes of sufferings will be erased.

– Ramcaritmanas

"If the Lord were to consider all my deeds, then I would know no redemption for at least 70 million lifetimes. (But) the Lord doesn't pay attention to the faults of his devotees. He is the friend of the suffering and of most gentle nature."

– Ramcaritmanas

The whole reason one does spiritual practices is to come to the realization that on our own, we can accomplish nothing. It is only then that we can surrender our ego and open our hearts to God.

– Swami Ramdas

Buddhism

Faith is of three kinds: blind faith, reasoned faith, and clear faith. Blind faith is not recommended. Reasoned faith is confidence gained through sound reasoning. Clear faith is confidence gained through experience.

The Relic

Once upon a time, in Tibet there was an old woman who was very religious. She had one son who was a trader, travelling back and forth from Tibet to India on business. The old woman was very keen on having a relic of the Buddha as the object of her devotions, so she asked her son to bring her a Buddha relic the next time he went to India.

The old woman's son travelled for six weeks by foot to India, buying and selling his wares along the way. After some months, he returned to Tibet. When he reached home, his mother asked him for the relic and was very sad when she found he had brought nothing.

The next year again the son travelled to India on business and just like before, his mother asked him to bring a relic of the Buddha with him when he returned to Tibet. After some months, he returned home, again without the relic.

The next year, when he again set out for India, his mother said, "This time for sure you must remember to bring me a relic of the Buddha for my religious devotions. If you do not, I shall commit suicide when you return." After some months, the son returned from his journey to India, but just as he was approaching his home, he realized that he had again forgotten his mother's request.

Fearing that his mother might indeed commit suicide if he returned home empty-handed for the third time, he decided he must take her something. Just at that moment, he saw a dog's tooth lying on the ground below him. Picking it up and dusting it off, he wrapped the dog's tooth in a beautiful silken cloth. When he reached home, he presented it to his mother, saying, "Here is the relic you requested—a tooth of the Buddha."

His mother, delighted, placed the tooth on the altar and began her religious devotions. From that day forth, the tooth emanated radiant, beautiful light in many colors that was seen by hundreds of people. Due to the old woman's faith, the tooth became an object of reverence that inspired religious devotion for miles around.

Zen Buddhism

If a pupil comes to a teacher simply to get a little skill in the art, the teacher finds his strong point, what comes most naturally to him as he now is, and develops that. It gives quick results and fulfills the end. But if someone comes who wants to master the art and give himself to it, the instruction is often the reverse. The teacher has to find out the weak points, and by special training bring them up to the level of the rest. Then he develops the whole range together. This kind of training produces in the pupil at various times a crisis of faith: faith in the teacher, and faith in himself. The teacher has to modify his instruction according to the fluctuating levels of faith.

Christianity

"Be not afraid; for behold, I bring you good news of a great joy . . . "
— *Bible, Luke 2:10*

"Remember the Sabbath day, to keep it holy."

— *Bible, Exodus 20:8*

"And I heard the voice of the Lord saying, 'Whom shall I send
and who will go . . . for us?' Then I said, 'Here I am, send me.'"
— *Bible, Isaiah 6:8*

The Woman Who Touched Jesus

The leader of a local synagogue, whose name was Jairus, came and fell down before Jesus, pleading with him to heal his little daughter.

"She is at the point of death," he said in desperation. "Please come and place your hands on her and make her live."

Jesus went with him, and a crowd thronged behind. In the crowd was a woman who had been sick for twelve years with a hemorrhage. She had suffered much from many doctors through the years and had become poor from paying them, and was no better but, in fact, was worse. She had heard all about the wonderful miracles Jesus did, and that is why she came up behind him through the crowd and touched his clothes.

For she thought to herself, "If I can just touch his clothing, I will be healed." And sure enough, as soon as she had touched him, the bleeding stopped and she knew she was well!

Jesus realized at once that healing power had gone out from him, so he turned around in the crowd and asked, "Who touched my clothes?"

His disciples said to him, "All this crowd pressing around you, and you ask who touched you?"

Character Education Year 1 Grades 6–12

But he kept on looking around to see who it was who had done it. Then the frightened woman, trembling at the realization of what had happened to her, came and fell at his feet and told him what she had done. And he said to her, "Daughter, your faith has made you well; go in peace, healed of your disease."

– Bible, Mark 5:22-34

Islam

The Messenger of Allah said: 'Islam has been built on five (Pillars): testifying that there is no God but Allah and that Muhammad is the Messenger of Allah; performing the prayers; paying regular charity; making the Pilgrimage to the (Sacred) House; fasting in Ramadan.'

– The Essential Teachings of Islam p 88
132: Hadith
Bukhari and Muslim (Agreed)

There are three things by which any one who possess these in him shall taste the sweetness of faith, namely, whoever loves God and His apostle more than anything besides them; whoever loves a servant (of God) only for (the sake of) God; and whoever is averse to return to infidelity after that God has saved him from it even as he would be averse to be flung into the fire (of hell).

– Selections from Mishkat-ul-masabi [211] p 49
Ana, BU: MU: TI: NA.

This is the Book (of Allah) without doubt. It is a guidance for God-fearing people who believe in the Unseen, keep up prayer and give from that which we have given them; who believe in the Book we have sent down to you as well as the Books we sent down before you; and who believe in their hearts in the life Hereafter. Such people are on the Path of their Lord and they shall prosper.

This is the answer to the opening request for Allah's guidance. Here is an end to doubt. The Divine Revelation of the Qur'an is indisputable, so we know that it contains no mistake. Here for all who wish to turn to Allah is the Path of Islam: belief in the one God; regular Prayer and Almsgiving; belief in the Holy Qur'an and the other Holy Books revealed through the Prophets; and belief in the Hereafter.

– The Essential Teachings of Islam p 2
2: The Cow (Baqara 2:2-5)

Chinese

"The Good Man rests content with Goodness, he that is merely wise pursues
  Goodness in the belief that it pays to do so."
                              — *Confucius*

"Here is the mystery of Virtue: it creates all and nourishes all; it directs all, but
  without conscious control."
                                  — *Lao Tzu*

Wealth and rank are what every man desires; but if they can only be retained to
the detriment of the Way he professes, he must relinquish them. Poverty and
obscurity are what every man detests; but if they can only be avoided to the
detriment of the Way he professes, he must accept them. The gentleman who
ever parts company with Goodness does not fulfill that name. Never for a
moment does a gentleman quit the way of Goodness. He is never so harried but
that he cleaves to this; never so tottering but that he cleaves to this.
                         — *The Analects, Book IV*

We look at it and see it not, though it is Omnipresent;
  and we name it the Root—balance.
We listen for it, and hear it not, though it is Omniscient;
  and we name it the Silence.
We feel for it, and touch it not, though it is Omnipotent;
  and we name it the Concealed.
These three Virtues have it; yet we cannot describe it as consisting of them;
  but mingling them aright, we apprehend the One.
                         — *Tao Te Ching*

Hawaii

Faithful Friends in the Forest

Lono was the chief of the big island of Hawaii. He was excited about making a trip to the
island of Kaua'i and seeing the famous Waimea Canyon, the many waterfalls, the beautiful
forests and beaches. He told his servants to get his canoe and belongings ready for the
journey. They obeyed his command but grumbled as they worked. Lono's servants did not like
having to go all that way to a strange place with strange gods.

The chief was so happy about making the trip he was not aware of the unhappiness of his
servants. As they neared the coast of Kaua'i he could not take his eyes off the beautiful green

                     Character Education Year 1 Grades 6–12

cliffs of the island. He encouraged his paddlers to pick up their pace, and as soon as the canoe landed on the beach he began asking people of Kaua'i, who had gathered to greet the strangers, where the canyon and the waterfalls were. He commanded his servants to tie up the canoe, bring his food and belongings, and follow him. He left the beach and began to hike at an eager and swift pace.

After a long time of climbing the trail he stopped to rest only to find that he was alone. When he looked back down the trail he saw only one man following after him. He realized in his haste he'd left all of his followers behind. He waited for the man and as he approached he saw that he was a stranger. "Who are you?" the chief asked. "I am Kapa'ihi of Kaua'i and I watched you land your canoe and then quickly leave it. Your followers watched you leave and then got back into the canoe when you were out of sight and paddled it back toward Hawaii. I thought you would need a guide and some food so I have brought some fish and poi. Let me serve you great chief."

"Those disloyal followers! They must be punished!" But as his eyes gazed at the beauty in the valley below him he was no longer angry. "Never mind them," he said, "I'm finally here on Kaua'i. Let's go see the sights I've longed to see." They climbed up the steep slopes for a long time and finally arrived at the edge of the canyon. He saw the stream which flowed far below them, it seemed so tiny next to the towering red walls of the canyon. He could see small white birds in the distance, they were the only moving sight for the viewer of such a glorious scene. Lono marveled at the breathtaking beauty of the canyon.

It was growing dark and a cool breeze came from the mountains and chilled the chief. Kapa'ihi gave him his own shoulder cape and led him to a cave which sheltered them from the wind. He knelt and served Lono the fish and poi and made a bed of dry grass, which he'd gathered, for them to sleep on.

Every day Lono and Kapa'ihi explored Kaua'i. They hiked over mountains, went into remote valleys and enjoyed the many waterfalls which plunged into fern embraced pools of fresh water where they could swim. They looked at the steep, green cliffs of the coast which rose straight up from the beach. They finished the fish and poi and then Kapa'ihi found banana, fern shoots, and pandanus fruit to feed them. They each wore a shoulder cape he made from leaves to protect them from the rain. Kapa'ihi always walked several steps behind the chief out of respect for his position and always served him his food on his knees.

One evening Lono realized that he had gone so many places and done so much with Kapa'ihi that he should no longer have him act as a servant toward him but rather as a friend and companion, which he truly had become. He became so fond of this humble and thoughtful man that he was determined to have him honored when he returned to his island of Hawaii.

When the chief finally returned from Kaua'i he immediately punished all the men who had deserted him and made Kapa'ihi his trusted assistant. The others were jealous of this stranger's high rank and tried to convince Lono that Kapa'ihi was not trustworthy. Lono replied, "Together we have traveled the mountains and valleys of Kaua'i, Kapa'ihi and I, together we have seen waterfalls and walked in the rain, together we have seen the amazing canyon and steep, green cliffs. He was always beside me through our travels, loyal and faithful and you tell me he can't be trusted?" The jealous ones knew it was useless to say anything more.

After Kapa'ihi had served the chief for a long time on Hawaii, he requested permission to return to Kaua'i to visit his family. Lono granted permission but asked Kapa'ihi to keep his trip brief for he was dependent on him for advice and companionship. Kapa'ihi returned to his home island. Soon after he heard rumors that Lono never wanted to see him again. The chief had heard stories from the jealous people about Kapa'ihi which he believed. Kapa'ihi did not believe that his dear friend would do this to him and he was saddened by these rumors. In his sadness he wrote a song recalling their time together traveling on Kaua'i and exploring the beauty of the island.

When he returned to Hawaii he was told by the guard that he was not allowed to enter the home of the high chief Lono, his friend. He was shocked and dismayed! The rumors were true. He slumped down beside the house and began to sing his song. Inside the chief heard the words of his friend and felt ashamed. Why had he believed the stories of others and doubted the faithfulness of his dear companion? He ran to the door and told the guard to bring Kapa'ihi into his home. The guard told him that Kapa'ihi had gone. As they looked toward the beach they saw him getting into his canoe and paddling away.

"Go after him and bring him back, quickly, go!" The guard obeyed but later returned saying that Kapa'ihi said, "Give my love to your chief but tell him that I cannot return because he has believed the lies of others and shut his door to me." Lono realized that he needed to apologize to Kapa'ihi himself for he had been wrong about his friend and had treated him badly.

Lono ordered his double canoe to be readied and followed Kapa'ihi. Soon they came to Kohala and saw a man sitting on the beach with his head bent in sorrow. Lono realized it was his faithful friend and went to him. He softly began to chant the words of the song that Kapa'ihi had created about their journey together. Kapa'ihi looked up and greeted his chief with a smile. The two men embraced affectionately and Lono vowed to never let lies come between them again.

India

Faith, Devotions, and Resignation

A milkmaid used to supply milk to a Brahmin priest living on the other side of a river. Owing to the irregularities of the boat service, she could not supply him milk punctually every day. Once, being rebuked for her coming late, the poor woman said, "What can I do? I start early from my house, but have to wait for a long time at the riverbank for the boatman and the passengers." The priest said, "Woman! We cross the ocean of life by uttering the name of God, and can't you cross this little river?" The simple-hearted woman became very glad at heart on learning this easy means of crossing the river. From the next day on, the milk was always supplied in the morning. One day the priest said to the woman, "How is it that you are no longer late?" She said, "I cross the river by uttering the name of the Lord as you told me to do, and I don't stand now in need of a boatman." The priest could not believe this and said, "Can you show me how you cross the river?" The woman took him with her and began to walk over the water. Looking behind, the woman saw the priest in a sad plight and said, "How is it, Sir, that you are uttering the name of God with your mouth, but at the same time with your hands you are trying to keep your cloth untouched by water? You do not fully rely on Him." Entire resignation and absolute faith in God are at the root of all miraculous deeds.

Judaism

The Precious Prayer

During Yom Kippur, Rabbi Isaac Luria was praying in a synagogue when an angel came and told him about a man whose words, when he prayed, reached the highest of heavens. The angel told him the name of the man and where he lived. When Yom Kippur was over, the rabbi made haste to find this man.

He searched the city for the man. First he went to the House of Study, then to the market, where he asked for information on the man with that name. He was told that the man lived in the mountains and was a poor farmer.

The rabbi set out for the mountains to find the farmer and was surprised when he found him that his house was just a poor hut. He was greeted by the farmer and invited into the hut. The rabbi asked him to tell him about his prayers. Surprised by the question, the man told the rabbi that he could not say prayers because he did not know how to read although he knew his alphabet.

Puzzled by this response, the rabbi asked the man what he did on Yom Kippur. The man replied that he had gone to the synagogue and had seen everyone praying. He felt heartbroken, so he recited the alphabet and asked that God take the letters and form them into a prayer which would rise like the scent of honeysuckle, for that was the sweetest scent he knew. The farmer said that he repeated this plea with all his strength over and over.

The rabbi understood what secret God had sent him to learn: that man sees only what is before his eyes, but God sees what is in the heart, which is what made the prayers of the farmer so precious.

Japanese

Jojofu

Long, long ago, there lived a fine young hunter named Takumi. Takumi hunted wild boar and deer in the mountains and kept about thirty hunting dogs, which he cared for dearly. He loved his dogs deeply; but of the thirty, there was one called Jojofu who was his favorite. She was not only the bravest, but the very smartest of the pack.

One day, Takumi set off with ten of his strongest dogs into the mountains. It was a good day for hunting. As usual, the dogs followed close behind Takumi as they climbed higher and higher into the woods—all but Jojofu. Takumi always let Jojofu remain at his side, as she feared nothing and could always signal Takumi against danger.

Takumi let Jojofu lead them through thick brush and over a rough path until they came to a grassy clearing. But rather than remain on the open grass where it would be easiest to walk, Jojofu darted immediately back into the dark woods. "Where are you taking us, silly dog? It is so much more difficult to make our way through the woods!"

But Jojofu continued to lead them into the trees, turning to bark an encouragement for them to follow. Takumi cried after her, "Jojofu! This is not the way! Come here!"

All at once, there was a great rumbling coming from the clearing behind them. Takumi turned to see huge boulders cascading down the hillside and tumbling onto the clearing they had just left. "A landslide," Takumi murmured. "We would have been buried there had it not been for Jojofu!" He called her to his side and said, "Forgive me for not trusting your eyes and ears, which are much sharper than my own."

The group moved on through thicker woods and a heavy gray mist hung over them, veiling their sight. Jojofu led them slowly and carefully as she felt for the safest trail. All of a sudden, she stopped. Takumi urged her on, but she would not budge. "We must continue, Jojofu, or we will not get to the hunting grounds before nightfall." Jojofu let out a sharp bark, then lay down at her master's feet, refusing to proceed. Impatient, Takumi called to one of his livelier dogs, Bakana. Bakana raced forward, bounding past Jojofu and Takumi into the heavy mist. Only seconds later did they hear a yelp and the sound of crashing stones and falling dirt. With fear and regret, Takumi picked up a long stick and felt his way through the mist. After only a few steps he felt where the path ended, and the ground dropped off suddenly at the edge of a treacherous cliff.

Takumi turned back to Jojofu and dropped to his knees. "Jojofu," he cried, "once again you have tried to lead me to safety. I promise I will never again lose faith in you whatever you do!"

By this time, the air had grown very crisp and night was falling, so Takumi decided to make camp. He built a large campfire and found a place to sleep in the broad branch of a tall tree. He knew he would be safe from the creatures in the forest if he were high off the ground, especially with Jojofu keeping guard below. So after a meal of fish and rice, he climbed up into his lofty bed and fell asleep.

A few hours later, a deep growl from Jojofu awoke Takumi. He rubbed the sleep from his eyes and looked down to see Jojofu staring up at him from below. Her eyes glared up at him through the darkness and she snarled viciously, baring her bright teeth.

"What's wrong, Jojofu? Can't you see it's only me up here? Now go to sleep, girl." Takumi called down to his dog.

With that, she lept up at the base of the tree, her front paws clawing at the bark, her eyes yellow with anger. Her lips curled back as she barked fiercely upward at Takumi. He saw the white froth at her mouth and became worried. "Could she have eaten a poisonous mushroom? What could have made her crazy like this?" Then, with great shock, he realized that none of the other dogs remained below. There was only Jojofu, gone wild, as Takumi had never seen her before. "Something is terribly wrong," thought Takumi, as Jojofu's rage seemed to build.

"She is mad!" thought Takumi, fearing for his own safety. Slowly, he drew out his sword, dreading what he thought he must do. The sword flashed in the moonlight, but Jojofu did not back away. Instead, she leapt higher and higher, getting closer to Takumi's branch with each bound. Afraid of her anger and strength, Takumi wondered whether he might have to kill his beloved companion in order to save himself. Then, he remembered the promise he had made at the cliff. He had said that no matter what, he would not lose faith in her. Even if she were mad, he would not turn against her. He slid his sword back into its sheath, took a deep breath, and jumped to the ground below.

In the same instant that he left his branch, Jojofu leapt high into the air and landed just where Takumi had made his bed. She snarled and clawed among the branches just above, then suddenly fell to the ground with a giant snake held between her powerful jaws. Takumi was terrified as Jojofu and the great beast thrashed about. Then, as if awakening suddenly from a nightmare, he drew his sword swiftly and killed the enormous snake.

He took Jojofu into his arms and cried, "Once more you have saved my life. I will trust you always, my beloved and faithful friend!" Just then, Jojofu broke out of Takumi's embrace and ran toward the lifeless serpent.

She sniffed at the snake's belly and began to bark and paw at it. "Is it still alive, girl?" Takumi asked nervously. Once again he drew his sword and struck at the creature's stomach. From the opening emerged all of Takumi's missing dogs. They ran to Jojofu, licking her face in gratitude.

Takumi never traveled without Jojofu beside him. Stories were told from village to village about the courageous hunter and his faithful companion who killed the huge serpent. Takumi told all he met of his trust in Jojofu, his eyes and ears.

PROVERBS AND MAXIMS

What you are is God's gift to you and what you do with what you are is your gift to God.
— *George Foster, Major League Outfielder*

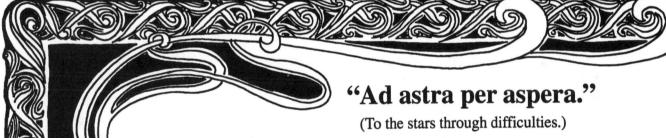

I'd hate to say my faith's a rock, but it's true. It is my strength; it gives me inner peace. Without my faith, I'd be in real bad shape. Faith gives a man hope, and hope is what life is all about. — *Tom Landry, NFL Coach*

"Ad astra per aspera."
(To the stars through difficulties.)

All the strength and force of man comes from his faith in things unseen. He who believes is strong; he who doubts is weak. Strong convictions precede great actions.
— *J. F. Clarke, Unitarian Clergyman*

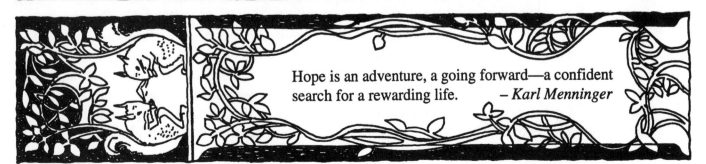

Hope is an adventure, a going forward—a confident search for a rewarding life. — *Karl Menninger*

HEROES AND HEROINES

JESUS (c. 3 B.C.E.–30 C.E.)

He was born in Bethlehem, Israel of humble Jewish parents, his father a carpenter and his mother a peasant teenager. Jesus grew up in relative obscurity learning his father's trade. He entered the public eye when he appeared at the River Jordan where John the Baptist was proclaiming the coming of the Messiah and baptizing people in the river as symbol of hope and new beginnings. John recognized Jesus as this new religious leader and baptized him. Jesus soon after began a three year period of teaching and healing around Galilee. He chose twelve men to travel with him, and rather than teach in the synagogues he preferred hillsides and river banks where the poor people could gather around him. Quoting from the Jewish law and prophets, he gave an interpretation that lifted up a new commandment of love. He taught with stories and parables and unintentionally challenged the religious authorities. He was accused of disturbing the peace, brought before Jewish and Roman tribunals and executed by crucifixion. His followers stayed together, forming a Jewish sect that became Christianity.

BUDDHA (c. 566–486 B.C.E.)

Born in Kapilavastu, Nepal, where his father ruled the Sakya tribe of the Gautama clan, he led the sheltered life of a young prince. He was married at age 16 and had one son. Tormented by the mysteries of illness, old age, and death he decided to leave his home, his riches, and his title to search for the truth. At the age of 29, he left the palace and traveled as a homeless holy man. He followed the teachings of two yoga masters without success and lived as an extreme ascetic for six years. Close to death and meditating on the mysteries of death and rebirth, the secrets were revealed to him, and he felt freed from all passions and all spiritual blindness. He gave his first sermon near Barnes in which the Four Noble Truths were outlined. He spent the rest of his life teaching and created a new order of itinerant monks. Worn out with age and exhaustion, he stopped in a forest near Kusinagori and, lying down between two trees, died peacefully, entering perfect nirvana.

KOBO DAISHI-KUKAI (774–835 C.E.)

Born in what is now Zentsuji City, Mao Kukai, the third son of Saeki Yoshimichi, was so bright and gifted his parents expected him to go into government service, which was the most respected profession at that time. He started his studies at the university in Kyoto, but he was more interested in searching for ultimate truth. A Buddhist monk introduced him to a practice of meditation called Kokugo-gumonjiho. As a result, he chose Buddhism and the priesthood rather than Confucianism and government bureaucracy. At age 19, in a cave at Cape Muroto, he attained a stage of enlightenment through his practice of meditation and made his final declaration to Buddhism. At age 31 he went to China and studied with Abbot Huikeo, the 7th patriarch of Esoteric Buddhism, who recognized immediately that Kukai would be his successor. After three months of study, Kukai was ordained the 8th patriarch of Esoteric Buddhism, and his master instructed him to return to Japan and spread the teachings and increase the happiness of the people there. He is credited with the founding of Japanese Buddhism. There are 3,000 folk tales and legends about this man who called himself Priest Kukai. In 921 he was canonized as Kobo Daishi; Daishi means great saint and Kobo means to spread.

LAO TZU (Third Century B.C.E.)

Three hundred years before the time of Confucius, a unique collection of people distilled the oral and written tradition of a thousand years into a work known as the *Tao Te Ching*. They lived along the Yellow River and in the remote valleys of north central China and were the descendants of a people who had a very advanced culture. Over several hundred years they had developed extensive written literature and produced many original philosophical thinkers. Sometime during the third century B.C.E., these people wrote the poems of the *Tao Te Ching*. Since there is no identifiable author it was necessary to invent one. By the time the *Tao Te Ching* was put into form, legend had provided an author, Lao Tzu—the old one or the old philosopher. Perhaps, Lao Tzu is the pseudonym or pen name of an ancient philosopher who was one of those reclusive mystics. *Tao Te Ching* translates as "The Book of the Way and Its Virtue" and is the basis of Taoism or The Way.

MUHAMMAD (c. 570–632 C.E.)

Born in Mecca, Muhammad was raised by a grandfather and an uncle. They took him into the family business of caravan trade. It was on one of their trips that he met some Nestorian monks, one of whom (Bahira) foretold his destiny as a prophet. Muhammed later became dissatisfied with the polytheism that was prevalent during that time and was especially displeased with the way the Ka'bah was being used for the worship of pagan idols. He was attracted to the monotheistic ideas being spread by Jews and Christians. He began regular retreats to a mountain cave and practiced long hours of asceticism and meditation. It was during one of these times in the year 610 that he had a dream that a book had been written in his heart. The dream was accompanied by the angel Gabriel and Muhammad became accustomed to receiving messages from God. He revealed these messages to a few disciples and after three years of revelations he was ordered to begin his public career. He proved to be a capable military and political leader and soon enjoyed absolute power. The complete Revelation is written down in the Koran and is complimented by a record of his oral teachings in the Hadith. Together they provide the basis for the faith of Islam.

PUT FAITH INTO ACTION

- Spend some time in meditation or prayer.

- Read something spiritual or religious.

- Put your trust in someone.

- Don't give up!

- Find something you can believe in beyond yourself.

COMMUNITY SERVICE IDEAS

- Organize a collection of toys, clothes, games for a local holiday project.

- Make Christmas cards for children who are sick.

- Adopt an underprivileged family for Christmas; rather than give presents to each other.

- Go Christmas caroling at a hospital or senior center.

- Volunteer at a local elementary school, doing tutoring, reading, arts and crafts, swimming, or teaching computers with children and youth.

- Broadcast the message of faith to your community by making posters to display in community centers, such as your local post office or grocery store.

- Invite to your class members of the community who are part of different religious groups. Ask them to share their faith with you.

- Take a survey of friends and neighbors to find out what people have faith in. Does everyone have some kind of true faith?

BOOKS ON FAITH

Chicken Sunday. Patricia Polocco. New York: Philomel Books, 1992.

The Judge: An Untrue Tale. Harve Zemach. New York: Farrar, Strauss and Giroux, 1969.

St. Francis of Assisi. Nina Bawden. New York: Lothrop, Lee & Shepard Books, 1983.

The Book of Virtues. William J. Bennett, ed. New York: Simon and Schuster, 1993.

    "Deucalion and Pyrrha" – p. 775

    "The Farewell Address" – p. 794

    "Going to Church" – p. 798

    "Hanukkah Hymn" – p. 765

    "The Honest Disciple" – p. 762

    "The Loom of Time" – p. 801

    "Nearer Home" – p. 769

    "Our Lady's Juggler" – p. 78

    "Second Inaugural Address" – p. 795

    "The Volunteer at Auschwitz" – p. 803

Commitment

SUPPORTIVE VALUES

Loyalty • Effort

DEFINITIONS

A pledge to a person, worthy goal, or concept.

Commitment is the state of being committed to a worthy goal, issue or concept. With commitment comes a pledge to uphold a promise, to fulfill an obligation, or to complete an involvement.

Loyalty is the quality of being faithful to one's commitments. A person who is faithful to their nation is a loyal citizen; while faithfulness to a promise means being loyal to a vow, faithfulness to a person means being a loyal friend, and faithfulness to responsibilities describes loyal conduct. Dedication, duty and devotion are good words to use in conjunction with this value.

Effort is deliberate exertion of mental, physical or spiritual power. This is where hard work enters the process. There are individuals who have taken the Puritan Work Ethic to an extreme and neglected their family and personal health in favor of work. However, there are other times when a sustained expenditure of effort is necessary to accomplish a definite goal. A willingness to work hard to fulfill commitments is deserving of high priority.

PURPOSE

Inherent in every person's life are certain roles that entail particular responsibilities. Some of these roles are given to us, such as son or daughter, while others are chosen, such as musician or athlete. A consideration of the value of commitment will encourage our students to keep their word, keep trying until their goal is reached, and follow through on previously selected aspects of respect, responsibility, compassion, and faith.

Commitment ———— January

Day One:
Write a definition of commitment in your own words. Compare your individual thoughts with the definitions provided on page 85.

Day Two:
Use the discussion questions on page 88 to continue thinking and learning about commitment.

Day Three:
Did you make a New Year's Resolution? If you did, share it with the class. It takes a lot of commitment to follow through on your resolution for an entire year. Try to make resolutions that are possible to keep and commit to keeping them.

Day Four:
Commitment to a goal means hanging in even when the goal seems impossible. Think of a time when you were committed to accomplishing a goal. (Learning to swim, memorizing a poem or finishing a very long book.) How did you feel when you finally reached that goal? Write about it.

Day Five:
Have you ever made a promise to do something for someone? (i.e. Clean your room or watch a younger sibling.) That's a commitment! Write or draw a journal entry to show the consequence of sticking to your promise.

Day Six:
Relationships take a lot of commitment to remain strong. Make a list of four people to whom you are willing to commit to being helpful during the coming week. Keep this list as a reminder of your commitment.

Day Seven:
Choose a bookmark from page 98. Decorate it and cut it out. Then give it to a friend or relative as a sign of your commitment to maintaining that relationship.

Day Eight:
Any type of long-term goal takes a lot of commitment. Choose and plan a community service project from page 100 or one appropriate to your community.

Day Nine:
Show your commitment as a class by following through with the service project.

Day Ten:
Discuss your service project and determine if it was as successful as it could have been. Were all members of the class committed to the project? What would you do differently if you were to plan and carry out another class service project?

Day Eleven:
Read a story about commitment from the selection on pages 89-97. Discuss what the story had to teach about the value of commitment.

Day Twelve:
Create and present an award to someone you know who has followed through on an important commitment during the past week.

Day Thirteen:
Rate on a scale from one (easiest) to ten (hardest) these acts of commitment. 1) Getting an A on your next test 2) Turning in all your homework on time 3) Making your bed every morning for a week 4) Telling your friends the truth 5) Learning how to play a new computer game.

Day Fourteen:
Becoming independent means taking responsibility to make a commitment to care for yourself. To be completely self-sufficient you need to provide certain things for yourself. Make a list of what you will need to provide to follow through on a commitment to take care of yourself.

Day Fifteen:
Is there something in your community that you would like to change for the better? Write down a list and then choose the one that is the most realistic and you feel you have the most commitment to. Write a letter encouraging yourself to follow through on this commitment everyday.

Day Sixteen:
Meet with a partner to compare your letters from yesterday. Then join a class discussion to determine three things your class as a whole could commit to making changes for the better.

Day Seventeen:
Team sports rely on each player's individual commitment to play his or her best. Team effort is key to a team success. Choose a team sport to examine as to how commitment can make all the difference.

Day Eighteen:
Read about the heroes and heroines whose stories are told on page 99. Discuss how each person was rewarded by his or her commitment.

Day Nineteen:
Make a banner or poster to post in the school cafeteria or library to remind students and visitors to the school of the importance of commitment to doing one's best everyday.

Day Twenty:
Review the lessons of commitment that you have learned this month. Reflect on how you can make a commitment now to embrace these values throughout your life.

COMMITMENT IN OTHER LANGUAGES

Chinese	*heng*	constant; regular; continually, persevering
	xin	heart; the moral nature; the mind; the affections; intention
French	*l'engagement*	to commit oneself to something or someone by means of a promise or contract; making a decision to get publicly involved in social or political problems
German	*verpflichtung*	obligation, duty, commitment
Hawaiian	*kupa'a*	"steadfast, firm, constant, immovable" (ku means "to stand" and pa'a means "firm solid")
Japanese	*chikai*	to promise with words
Korean	*yak sok*	pledge
Latin	*pignus*	commitment
Spanish	*compromiso*	commitment, obligation, duty
Tagalog	*panata*	a promise, pledge or vow; promising to fulfill a certain duty with religious devotion

DISCUSSION QUESTIONS

- Share examples to which people are committed (the nation, vows of marriage, their work, family, volunteer work).

- What are the signs of their commitment?

- Are there levels of commitment?

- Is there a danger in being partly or halfway committed to something?

- What are some of the duties you have accepted for yourself?

- What duties have been imposed upon you?

- Is it possible to like or enjoy a duty or obligation? How?

- How would you describe someone who works hard? Would you describe them as focused . . . as working long hours . . . as someone who concentrates?

- Is *lazy* the opposite of *hard-working*?

- Is there anything in between?

- Where does leisure time come in?

- Are you described as determined, dedicated, or devoted?

STORIES AND THOUGHTS FROM SPIRITUAL TRADITIONS

Hinduism

You have the right to work, but for the work's sake only. You have no right to the fruits of work. Desire for the fruits of work must never be your motive in working. Never give way to laziness, either.

Perform every action with your heart fixed on the Supreme Lord. Renounce attachment to the fruits. Be even-tempered in success and failure; for it is this evenness of temper which is meant by yoga.

Work done with anxiety about results is far inferior to work done without such anxiety, in calm of self-surrender. Seek refuge in the knowledge of Brahman. They who work selfishly for results are miserable.

In the calm of self-surrender you can free yourself from the bondage of virtue and vice during this very life. Devote yourself, therefore, to reaching union with Brahman. To unite the heart with Brahman and then to act: that is the secret of non-attached work. In the calm of self-surrender, the seers renounce the fruits of their actions, and so reach enlightenment. Then they are free from the bondage of rebirth, and pass to that state which is beyond all evil.

– Bhagavad Gita

Never promise anything unless you are willing to die in order to fulfill it.

– Tradition

One who takes a virtuous vow has the strength of seven generations to help him succeed. One who breaks a vow brings ill fortune on seven generations.

– Tradition

Buddhism

Commitment, or joyful effort, overcomes all obstacles, especially laziness and procrastination.

The Buddha described four kinds of effort. First is to prevent unwholesome states of mind from arising. Second is to eliminate unwholesome thoughts when they arise. Third is to generate wholesome states of mind. Fourth is to further develop wholesome thoughts when they arise. We can practice this as we pay attention to our breathing.

Asanga Learns a Lesson

There was once a yogi named Asanga who made a determination to meditate ceaselessly in a mountain cave until he achieved a vision of Manjushri, the bodhisattva of wisdom. He practiced and practiced with all his might, but after three years had achieved no realization at all. Discouraged about not getting results from his practice, he decided to leave his cave. As he was walking out of his cave, he noticed an indentation in the rock cliff above his head. Curious, he stood wondering how this indentation came about. As he stood wondering, suddenly a wild bird flew past, carrying morsels of food to feed her young. As she flew past, her wing brushed against the rock. Astonished, Asanga realized that the indentation in the rock had been created by the frequent rubbing of the bird's wing against the rock. See that, Asanga thought, "If a bird is so diligent in feeding her young that her feathered wing rubs a dent in rock, shouldn't I be even more diligent in my meditation?" With that, he reentered his cave and sat down to practice again.

Three more years went by, but Asanga still did not achieve the realization he was seeking. Feeling frustrated, once more he decided to give up the practice and left the cave. On the way out, he noticed an impression in the stone in front of the cave. Curious how it got there, he stood watching until he realized it was created by the ceaseless drip of water from the ledge above. Observing this he thought, "If drops of water falling repeatedly on stone can carve an impression in stone, eventually my practice must bear fruit." So he returned to his cave and made a renewed commitment to practice conscientiously.

Three more years went by, but Asanga still had not attained realization. By this time, he was completely fed up, so he left his cave and headed down the mountain. When he came to the road, he saw an old man rubbing a piece of metal with a cloth. "What are you doing?" he asked. "I'm making a needle," answered the old man. "How long have you been at it?" he queried. "Three years," said the old man. Seeing the old man's persistence, Asanga thought, 'Even for the trivial purpose of making a needle, this man has been rubbing away diligently for three years. Shouldn't I, who seek the goal of highest enlightenment, exert far more effort than that?" So he went back to his cave to continue his practice.

Three years later, even after a full 12 years of meditation, he still had not reached his lofty goal of spiritual realization, so he thought, 'This is hopeless. I give up,' and headed down from the mountain and into the town. Just as he reached the edge of town, he stopped abruptly at the sight of a dog whose wounded leg was being eaten away by maggots. Moved by great compassion, he decided to remove the maggots one by one from the wound. 'But how to move the maggots without harming them?' he thought.

Finally he resolved to lift the maggots from the dog's wound with his tongue to keep from harming them. He leaned down toward the wound, but his tongue touched only earth. And there before him stood Manjushri, the bodhisattva of wisdom. Asanga was stunned and said, "Where have you been? I have been meditating 12 years to achieve a vision of you, but in vain." And Manjushri said, "I have been with you all along, but you were not able to see me. Only now, through the merit of your great compassion for the suffering of these living creatures have you gained the insight to behold me. If you don't believe me, put me on your shoulder and take me through the town." And sure enough, as he walked through the town with Manjushri perched on his shoulder, only one person noticed and it was an old woman who saw a dog draped over his shoulder. Finally, through the insight born of compassion, Asanga's diligent practice had come to fruition.

Zen Buddhism

To turn within means all the twenty-four hours and in every situation, to pierce one by one through the layers covering the self, deeper and deeper, to a place which cannot be described. It is when thinking comes to an end and making distinctions ceases, when wrong views and ideas disappear of themselves without having to be driven forth, when without being sought the true action and true impulse appear of themselves. It is then one can know what is the truth of the heart.

The man resolute in the way must from the beginning never lose sight of it, whether in a place of calm or in a place of strife, and he must not be clinging to quiet places and shunning those where there is disturbance. If he tries to take refuge from trouble by running to some quiet place, he will fall into dark regions.

If when he is trying to throw off delusions and discover truth, everything is a whirl of possibilities, he must cut off the thousand impulses and go straightforward, having no thought at all about good or bad; not hating the passions, he must simply make his heart pure.

Christianity

"For we have seen his star in the East and have come to worship him."
— *Bible, Matthew 2:26*

"For where you go I will go, and where you lodge I will lodge; your people shall be my people and your God my God."
— *Bible, Ruth 1:16*

"Present your bodies as a living sacrifice, holy and acceptable to God, which is your spiritual worship."
— *Bible, Romans 12:1*

Islam

I obtained the blessing of kissing the master's feet. One of those present told the story of a man who was extremely virtuous, and also eager to enter the service of dervishes. I told him: "Why do you not attach yourself to the master (i.e., Shaykh Nizam ad-din)?" He replied: "I once went there with the intention of professing the oath of allegiance to him. When I saw the spread out tablecloths and the burning candles, however, I decided to direct my commitment elsewhere, and left."

The master—may God remember him with favor—on hearing this story, turned to those present and asked: "Where are these tablecloths? Where are the candles?" Then he smiled and added: "Since the time was not right for him to benefit from the oath of allegiance, they appeared to him just as he described them." At this point the servant interjected: "Why would tablecloths and candles be THE BASIS FOR directing one's COMMITMENT elsewhere?" On his blessed lips came this response: "Some make a commitment on very trivial grounds; others bring to discipleship a firm faith and unshakable constancy."

– Nizam Ad-Din Awliya: Morals of the Heart p 107-8
I. Assembly 25
Friday, the 9th of Ramadan, A.H. 708 (1 March 1309)

"Prosper" in the spiritual sense, for that is all that matters, as the life of his world is brief and fleeting, and of small account as against Eternity.

– The Meaning of the Holy Qur'an p 258
5:35

Chinese

"In your promises cleave to what is right, and you will be able to fulfill your word. In your obeisances cleave to ritual, and you will keep dishonor at bay."   *– Confucius*

"A gentleman covets the reputation of being slow in word but prompt in deed."

– Confucius

Of Tzu-chan the master said that in him were to be found four of the virtues that belong to the Way of the true gentleman. In his private conduct he was courteous, in serving his master he was punctilious, in providing for the needs of the people he gave them even more than their due; in exacting service from the people, he was just.

– The Analects, Book V

Jan Chau said, It is not that your way does not commend itself to me, but that it demands powers I do not possess. The Master said, He whose strength gives out collapses during the course of the journey (the Way); but you deliberately draw the line.

– The Analects, Book VI

India

God Never Fails

Nothing is omitted from the Gita that the unconsoled heart requires. There are even the tender promises of daily bread, so dear to the anxious: "They who depend on Me, putting aside all care, whatsoever they need, I myself carry it to them," runs one verse. Of this a beautiful story is told in the villages.

A Brahmin sat copying the text, but when the word "carry" had been written, he felt a doubt. "My dear," he said, turning to consult his wife, "thinkest thou not it is irreverent to say 'carry' here? Did not our Lord mean 'send'?" "Beyond doubt, beloved," answered his wife, "it is as thou sayest. Let the word be 'send'." Then the man took his penknife and erased the word he had just written, substituting his own emendation for it. A moment later he rose up to go and bathe. But his wife stood before him with a troubled face. "I told thee not," she said, "that there is no food in the house, and nought have I to cook for thee." The Brahmin smiled gently. "Let us call upon our Lord to fulfill His own promise;" he replied quietly. "Meantime, I shall go and bathe," and he passed into the next room. Hardly a few minutes had passed when his wife was called to the door by a beautiful youth who stood there with a basketful of delicious food, ready for eating. "Who sent me this?" the woman asked in amazement. "Your husband called me to carry it," said the lad carelessly, putting the basket, as he spoke, into her hands. But to her horror, as he lifted his arms, the housewife noted cuts and gashes above his heart. "Alas, my poor child, who hath wounded thee?" she cried.

"Your husband, before he called me, cut me with a small sharp weapon," was the quiet answer. Dumb with astonishment, the Brahmin's wife turned away to bestow the viands he had brought, and when she came back to the door the youth had gone. At that instant her husband re-entered the room, having returned, as she supposed from bathing. Her wonder about the food was forgotten in indignant sympathy. "Why," she cried, "didst thou so hurt the messenger?" The man looked at her without understanding. "Him whom thou sentest to me with food, as thou didst go to bathe," she explained. "To bathe!" he stammered, "I have not yet been!" Then the eyes of husband and wife met, and they both knew who had come to them, and how they had wounded the heart of the Lord. And the Brahmin returned to the sacred text, and once more erasing the word restored it to its original form, for there can be no doubt that the true reading is, "They who depend on Me, putting aside all care, whatsoever they need, I myself carry it to them." Such was the faith in God in ancient India, and even today that faith does live in the hearts of the peasants.

Judaism

The Sock Maker

The Baal Shem, was in a town in which he was staying briefly, when he observed a man walking by his house one morning before prayer time. The man seemed very intent on his mission and had his prayer shawl and his ritual leather ties containing scripture with him. When the Baal Shem asked his host about the man he was told that the man was a sock maker and that he went to the House of Prayer every day of every season of every year. The Baal Shem asked someone to tell the man that he wanted some of his socks. Soon the man came to show him his goods which were of sheep's wool and well made. When asked how much the man wanted for one pair of socks he replied, "One and a half gulden." The rabbi said, "Then you will be satisfied with one gulden." The sock maker responded, "I would've said one gulden if I would be satisfied with one gulden." The rabbi quizzed him about how he spent his days to which he replied, "Making socks." He went on to explain that he made about forty or fifty pairs then he'd press them until they were the right shape. Merchants would come to his house to buy his socks and he never had to leave home. The only reason he left his home today was to honor the Baal Shem. The rabbi asked him what he did in the morning before he went to prayer.

"I make socks."

"And what psalms do you recite?"

"When I am working I recite the psalms which I know."

When the sock maker went home, the Baal Shem said to his disciples who surrounded him, "Today you have seen the cornerstone which will support the Temple until the Messiah arrives."

West Indian

The Faithful Friend

Once upon a time, on the island of Martinique, there lived a wealthy man. Unfortunately, this gentleman's beloved wife had died giving birth to their only son, Clement, and so the gentleman hired a widow from a nearby town to care for his child. Now the French-born widow had a son of her own named Hippolyte.

The two boys grew up like brothers and loved each other dearly. They enjoyed the same games and books. They both grew to be tall and handsome, Clement with skin the deep color of cocoa, and Hippolyte with fair skin only lightly tanned by the tropical sun.

One day, Clement showed his friend a small painting of a young woman. "This is Pauline. She is Monsieur Zabocat's niece. I am in love with her. I am going to journey to her home in Macouba in order to ask her uncle for her hand in marriage. Will you come with me, dear friend?" asked Clement of Hippolyte.

Now, Hippolyte had heard tales of Monsieur Zabocat who was thought to be a wizard of sorts. He knew that there was a good deal of mystery surrounding Monsieur Zabocat and that Clement's journey might prove dangerous. Yet, he could see the happiness in his friend's face when he spoke of Pauline. He did not want to disappoint Clement by mentioning Monsieur Zabocat's wizardry so he agreed to go. "As long as my dear friend is happy," thought Hippolyte, "then I am happy," and they set off for Macouba the next day.

The sun was blazing in the brilliant blue sky and the men were excited to be on their journey. All around them were the fragrant blossoms and luscious fruit of the island. Their adventure had begun happily. But just as they approached Macouba, they discovered a beggar sick and suffering in the heat along the side of the path. "We cannot leave that poor man this way," said Hippolyte. "Let us carry him into the shade of the banana grove and give him something to drink."

The two young men lifted the weakened man into the grove and placed him in the cool shade of a tree. There they gave him food and drink and stayed until they were sure of his comfort. Although it was much later in the day when they set off again, they were happy to have been of help.

Finally, at twilight, they reached Monsieur Zabocat's large estate. Clement was flushed with excitement, yet Hippolyte remained wary. At last they met the master of the House. "Good evening, sir," said Clement as he introduced himself and his good friend. Hippolyte noticed the warm glances cast between Clement and Pauline, as well as the cool stare of Pauline's uncle, Monsieur Zabocat.

After the young men spoke of their journey, Monsieur Zabocat invited them to stay for dinner out of respect for Clement's father, although his manner remained cold. Servants set the table with fine china and silver and the meal which followed was exquisite. There was spicy soup, and fresh crab, there were rich sweets and luscious fruit. At the end of the meal, Clement could wait no longer to declare his love for Pauline. He knelt before her and asked her to marry him.

When she accepted, her uncle grew furious. "I forbid it!" he declared. "I shall decide when and whom you shall marry and that is that!"

But Pauline was just as devoted to Clement as he was to her. "Dear uncle," she began, "I am so grateful for all you have done for me. But I am old enough to know my heart and I will marry Clement."

This outraged Monsieur Zabocat. In anger he swept the fine dishes from the table. "Then get out! None of you are welcome any longer!" The three young people rose to leave. Monsieur Zabocat raised his finger toward them, "But take care," he said in a low voice, "you are not married yet! We shall see if your marriage is to be." His eyes were fierce and the young people fled quickly so as not to anger him any more.

The moon was high in the night sky as they left Monsieur Zabocat's mansion. Pauline could not help weeping over her uncle's cruel words. Clement could not bear to see his beloved so unhappy. "Do not be sad. We are together and my father will welcome you with open arms when we arrive home. I am certain he will make peace with your uncle."

Clement's words soothed Pauline, and as they walked into the night the three talked and laughed until they became weary and stopped to sleep beneath some trees. But Hippolyte was troubled by an unnatural silence around them until all at once he heard the beating of drums in the dark distance. While his friends slept, he ventured into the forest. The sound of the drums led him to a clearing where he came upon three beautiful women. Hippolyte hid as he listened to the first woman say, "The lovely young girl and the handsome young man are asleep." The second woman nodded, "Yes, it is time for us to do what the great wizard Zabocat called us to do!" With that, the third woman cried out, "The spell must begin!"

Hippolyte was trembling as he realized that no matter how beautiful they were, these must be evil spirits summoned by Monsieur Zabocat to keep Pauline and Clement from getting married. He hoped they would not discover him as he continued to listen.

"Tomorrow, early in the morning, the couple will arrive at a stream." said the first woman.

"They will be so very thirsty and will drink from it," said the second.

"And then they shall die," confirmed the last. Then she added in a low voice, "If anyone should repeat this plan, his legs will turn to stone." The women vanished into the darkness, and Hippolyte crept back to watch over his friends.

When morning finally arrived, the others awoke and Hippolyte urged them to continue the journey quickly. He knew he could say nothing of what he had heard the night before. Before long, they did indeed come upon a stream. "Oh, let us have a drink," said Pauline, "before we go on our way." Hippolyte scooped up the murky water saying, "This water is not at all suitable for drinking. I fear it would make you very ill." In spite of their thirst, they walked on.

In the heat of midday, they paused to rest. While Pauline and Clement cooled themselves beneath the shade of a tree, Hippolyte scouted the area for any sign of the wicked ladies. He spotted them nearby in a grove of mango trees. "This time we shall not fail," said the first lady as she passed a ripe mango to the second one. "They will soon come upon this grove," cackled the second as she handed the fragrant fruit to the third lady. "Yes!" cried the third, "And they will eat the fruit and die!" She glanced around and added, "If anyone should tell of this plan, he will turn to stone up to his chest."

Once again, the women vanished and Hippolyte returned stealthily to his friends. When he found them, they were eager to start off on their journey. After only a few moments, they came upon the mango grove. Pauline was so anxious to eat the fruit but Hippolyte stopped her. He picked one and pretended to take a bite and spit it out. "It's terrible!" he said, grimacing. "Surely, these mangoes are poisonous!" he cried as he tossed the fruit away. Sadly, Pauline turned away from the trees and the three continued on.

As the day grew hotter, the friends stopped on the roadside to cool themselves. Ever vigilant, Hippolyte wandered restlessly near the forest. Once again, he came upon the evil women.

"We shall not be foiled this time," murmured the first of the ladies. "Once the young couple enters the house, they shall die."

"Ah yes," agreed the second, "on their wedding night they shall be stung by a serpent."

"And if anyone tells of this plan, he shall turn to stone from head to toe!" cried the third as she pulled a writhing serpent from her pocket just before the three of them disappeared once again. Hippolyte slipped off to rejoin his friends and hasten them on their way.

At long last, the trio arrived at the home of Monsieur Duforce. Happy to see the group, Monsieur Duforce welcomed them warmly and expressed his great joy over his son's engagement to the lovely Pauline. He assured them that he would set things right very soon with her uncle.

A few days later Monsieur Zabocat did, in fact arrive, saying that he would attend the wedding and that he had forgiven the couple. But Hippolyte, after all he had witnessed on their journey remained suspicious. In spite of Monsieur Zabocat's smiles and pleasant manner, Hippolyte sensed a viciousness which was terrifying. He watched and waited for the horrible serpent to appear but it did not.

The day of the wedding arrived. The couple looked more glorious than ever, Clement in a fine dark suit, and Pauline in a flowing white satin gown. Friends gathered excitedly at the home eager to celebrate the happiness of the young couple. As guests flocked to the garden to toast the bride and groom, Hippolyte hurriedly sharpened his cutlass inside, preparing to protect his dear friends against the worst. As soon as the couple entered the house, the huge deadly serpent appeared as if from nowhere. Writhing quickly toward the couple it raised its head to attack. At that very moment, Hippolyte lunged at the creature, striking it with his sharpened cutlass, and to everyone's shock the horrible serpent vanished into thin air.

People had gathered to witness the terrifying event and from amongst them Monsieur Zabocat cried out, "Hippolyte is jealous of his friend's happiness. He brandishes the sword with which he tried to harm the newlyweds!" Hippolyte knew he could not reveal what he had learned in the forest lest he turn to stone, so he had no choice but to gaze sadly at his friends. Stunned, Pauline and Clement did not know what to make of their dear friend's silence. "You have nothing to say for yourself, do you?" Monsieur Zabocat continued loudly. "You could not bear their happiness, so you were going to strike them both down with your cutlass!"

Hippolyte could no longer stand to see the sadness and confusion in the eyes of his treasured friends. He began to tell of his first encounter with the wicked women. As he spoke, his legs turned to stone.

"Stop! You need tell us no more," pleaded Clement. But Hippolyte wanted his friend to know the whole truth and continued to tell him about the deadly mangoes. Immediately, his body hardened up to his chest.

"Please, dear Hippolyte, say no more!" implored Pauline. But Hippolyte was driven out of faithfulness to his friends. As he finished his story, he turned completely to stone from head to toe.

At that moment, an old man moved forward from the crowd.

"I can bring him back to life on one condition," spoke the old man softly.

"Anything," said Clement eagerly,"I will do anything."

"You must take this curse upon yourself. Only then can I release your friend," the old man explained.

"I shall do it gladly. For he has saved my life many times over," said Clement as he embraced his new bride.

"Very well," said the old man and he waved his hand before the stone face of Hippolyte then blew gently over him.

At once, Hippolyte came to life again, but before he could say a word the old man moved to touch Clement with the tip of his finger. Monsieur Zabocat leaned forward eager to see the young man he detested turn to stone. Suddenly, the old man turned in the direction of none other than Monsieur Zabocat and touched him with his outstretched finger. It was Monsieur Zabocat who was turned to stone!

The old man looked kindly at Clement. "The spell was broken by your eagerness to give your own life for your friend's. The kindness you show to others returns to you." He smiled and in the next instant disappeared.

Clement and Hippolyte turned to look at one another in amazement. "Was that not the same poor man we helped along the roadside at the beginning of our journey?" asked Clement. Hippolyte shook his head. "Surely it couldn't be," he replied. "Or could it?" he wondered again. The two friends shrugged, smiled warmly at each other and embraced.

In the time that followed, Clement and Pauline lived very happily and Hippolyte fell in love and married, as well. The friends remained true and dear to each other always.

As for the statue of Monsieur Zabocat, it was placed in a corner of the garden where it quickly turned to dust.

PROVERBS AND MAXIMS

Concerning all arts of initiative and creation there is one elementary truth, the ignorance of which kills countless ideas and splendid plans: that the moment one definitely commits oneself, then Providence moves, too. All sorts of things occur to help one, that otherwise would never have occurred.
— *W. H. Murray*

People can be divided into three groups: those who make things happen, those who watch things happen, and those who wonder what happened. Showing up is 80 percent of life. — *Woody Allen*

"Aut viam inveniam aut faciam."
(Where there's a will, there's a way.)

The important thing in life is to try to be your best. Be honest with yourself and make an honest commitment to yourself, your family, your friends, and your community. An honest commitment means 100 percent. It means self-discipline, it means loyalty, and it means being able to be counted on in the clutch.
— *Joe Paterno, College Football Coach*

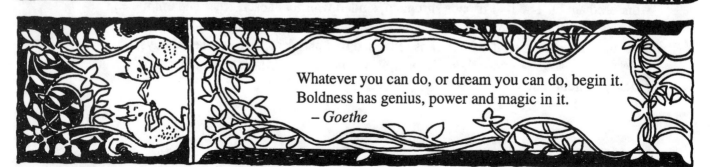

Whatever you can do, or dream you can do, begin it.
Boldness has genius, power and magic in it.
— *Goethe*

HEROES AND HEROINES

EARL E. BAKKEN (1924–)

Born in Minneapolis, Minnesota, he was educated in the Columbia Heights public schools and the University of Minnesota with a degree in electrical engineering. Earl was always fascinated with electricity; while he was a teenager, he made a robot that could smoke cigarettes. At age nine, when he saw the original *Frankenstein* movie, he decided he wanted to make electrical instruments that could help people. He co-founded Medtronic, Inc. in 1949 and in 1957 developed the first wearable, external, battery-powered, transistorized pacemaker. This pacemaker has developed through several revisions and is used by millions of people. His medical devices have transformed and saved millions of lives. Retiring in Waimea, Hawaii, he heads the Board of Directors of the North Hawaii Community Hospital. Already recognized as a center for healing, it emphasizes a balance of technology and medical innovations with the human touch and spirituality. His work embodies a lifetime commitment to human service and healing.

DIANE FOSSEY (1932–1985)

Born in San Francisco, California, she graduated from San Jose State College in 1954 with a degree in occupational therapy. She worked for several years in a children's hospital in Kentucky; then, in 1963, inspired by the writing of American zoologist George B. Schaller, she traveled to Africa. She visited the British anthropologist Louis Leakey and observed mountain gorillas. These encounters changed her life completely, and she stayed in Africa. She became an astute and patient observer of gorilla behavior, knew each as an individual, and regarded them as gentle social animals. She established the Karisoke Research Center in 1967, which became an international center for gorilla research. She spent twenty-two years studying the ecology and behavior of the mountain gorilla, and her book *Gorillas in the Mist* (1983) recounts much of this research. In 1985 she was found murdered at her campsite; some authorities believe she was killed because of her efforts to stop the poaching of gorillas. As a result of her research and conservation efforts, the mountain gorillas are protected by the government of Rwanda and by the international conservation and scientific communities.

VINCE LOMBARDI (1913–1970)

Born in Brooklyn, New York as the first of five children of an Italian immigrant, Vince was raised in a strict Catholic environment. He studied for the priesthood for two years, but changed his mind and his school. He majored in business at Fordham University and starred on the football team as a guard, where he was a member of the famous "Seven Blocks of Granite." In 1939, while studying law in night school, he took a job as a high school teacher and assistant football coach. He quickly moved from this small beginning to Fordham and then to West Point, where he developed his basic coaching philosophy. He was hired by the New York Giants as an offensive coach and earned the reputation of a coach who could take a poorly performing team and produce a winner. In 1958 he became head coach of the Green Bay Packers, where his philosophy and success became legendary.

PUT COMMITMENT INTO ACTION

- Renew your commitment to something you've been doing halfway for a few weeks or months.

- Write a letter of thanks to a local or national politician who has done a good job with one of his/her duties.

- Volunteer for a community service project.

- Commit yourself to a local cause for at least one year.

COMMUNITY SERVICE IDEAS

- Commit to an ongoing project with a community agency: taking them toys and books, making holiday decorations, going for visits and singing to them.

- Tutor a younger student.

- Volunteer at a children's day care center or at a hospital.

- Volunteer to sort and pack donations at a charitable organization.

- Volunteer to process books at a local library.

- Remind your community of the importance of commitment by creating signs to hang up in public buildings.

- Decide with your family to commit to a specific "family night" for each week for a month.

BOOKS ON COMMITMENT

Harald and the Great Stag. Donald Carrick. New York: Clarion Books, 1988.

King's Fountain. Lloyd Alexander. New York: Dutton, 1971.

Many Lives of Chio and Goro. Betty Jean Lifton. New York: W.W. Norton, 1968.

Moss Gown. William Hooks. New York: Clarion Books, 1987.

Sir Gawain and the Loathly Lady. Selina Hastings. New York: Lothrop, Lee & Shepard Books, 1985.

The Book of Virtues. William J. Bennett, ed. New York: Simon and Schuster, 1993.

"Abraham Lincoln Denies a Loan" – p. 402

"The Bundle of Sticks" – p. 388

"The Commercial Artist" – p. 140

"The Farmer and His Sons" – p. 370

"Penelope's Web" – p. 701

"The Thousandth Men" – p. 736

"Tom Sawyer Gives Up the Brush" – p. 398

"The Village Blacksmith" – p. 397

"Washington Rejects a Crown" – p. 717

SUPPORTIVE VALUES

Friendship • Sincerity

DEFINITIONS

Unselfish kindly concern for the good of another.

Love is probably the most written about subject in the world. The question of what love really is has always been a mystery. M. Scott Peck writes, "Love is too large, too deep ever to be truly understood or measured or limited within the framework of words." Henry Drummond refers to love as the summum bonum—the supreme good. Drummond points out that in a letter to the Corinthians, Paul wrote, "Now abide Faith, Hope, Love, these three; but the greatest of these is Love." Paul also wrote, "Love is the fulfilling of the law." It is the highest of rules, Drummond contends: "It is the rule for fulfilling all rules, the new commandment for keeping all the old commandments . . . " Much has been written about the kinds of love which can be felt: filial or brotherly love, erotic or romantic love, and agape which is an unselfish interest and care for the welfare of another. Agape is the kind of love to which we are referring as the value for this month.

Friendship fits our above definition of love and the **sincerity** with which we express our feelings for each other is important. Too often we express our friendly feelings in insincere ways. Sincerity connotes honesty and challenges us all to be more honest in our dealings with people.

PURPOSE

Sarcasm is a common mode of expression and regardless of how witty we think we may be, the real risk of hurting another remains. Sarcasm is the antithesis of sincerity. It is, as Ambrose Bierce remarked, " . . . the questionable weapon of questionable intellects." Again our emphasis on respect and The Golden Rule in our first month is a logical explanation for being more cautious of our use of sarcasm in class. Affirmation and encouragement would better exemplify how we can care for others in more sincere, friendly, and loving ways.

Love

Day One:
Look up in the dictionary the word love. Compare it with the meaning of the word love as you would describe it in your own words.

Day Two:
Sometimes it is difficult to love certain people. Discuss with a partner or in small groups ways to love people whom it is hard to love.

Day Three:
What is the difference between romantic love and platonic love? (If you don't know the meaning of platonic, look it up in the dictionary!) Write a short story and include examples of each type of love.

Day Four:
Discuss with your classmates whether animals feel love. Support your argument with your own experiences. Do some research to see if scientists have a theory on whether or not animals feel love.

Day Five:
Explain in a journal entry your understanding of what unconditional love is.

Day Six:
Work in small groups to discuss the questions on page 106 to gain a better understanding of love.

Day Seven:
In a total class setting, read the stories about love on page 107-111. What do these stories say about love. Discuss the implications of the stories and agree or disagree with the messages they convey.

Day Eight:
Brainstorm a list of ways to show love at school or at home. Pick one and find a time during the day to put that act of love into action.

Day Nine:
Write a journal entry about following through with your act of love yesterday. Tell how the other person seemed to feel when he or she received your love.

Day Ten:
Plan a field trip to share your love. Choose a site such as a home for the bed-ridden elderly or a children's hospital.

Day Eleven:
Prepare for your field trip by making the bookmarks on page 121. Try to have them laminated after you have colored and cut them out.

Day Twelve:
Go on your field trip. Sing a song or tell the residents a story. Pass out the bookmarks so that they will have a reminder that they are loved!

Day Thirteen:
Reflect on your trip. How did it make you feel to share your love? Write a poem about your experience.

Day Fourteen:
Explore in a small group the meaning of self-love. Is it important to love yourself? Why? Share one thing about yourself that you feel is worthy of love. Then go around the group and share one thing about each person in the group that you love.

Day Fifteen:
As a class, choose an activity from page 115 and do it.

Day Sixteen:
Pick a community service project from page 116 and plan to put it into action.

Day Seventeen:
Follow through on your community service project.

Day Eighteen:
Select a book with a theme about love and share it with a younger child.

Day Nineteen:
Hold a class election to select a Queen and King of Hearts. These people should be the ones who most consistently represented the true value of love throughout the month.

Day Twenty:
Reflect on what you learned this month about love. Commit to embracing love as a life long value.

LOVE IN OTHER LANGUAGES

Chinese	*ai*	to love; to be fond of; to like; love and affection
French	*l'amour*	an interior movement of devotion directed towards God, an ideal, another person; a very strong emotion or attachment involving tenderness and physical attraction between two people (In Switzerland "les amours" are the last drops of a bottle of wine!)
German	*liebe*	love, affection, kindness, passion, charity
Hawaiian	*aloha*	love, affection
Japanese	*ai*	a merciful mind that gives people food
Korean	*sa rang*	amour
Latin	*amor*	from Old Norse "lofa" (to love); related to Latin "libere" (to be pleasing) (something pleasing)
Spanish	*amor*	love, affection
Tagalog	*pagmamahal*	to have a fond, deep, tender feeling toward someone

DISCUSSION QUESTIONS

• Is it easy to talk about love? Why?

• Are there other words you would rather use than love? What are they?

• Are they a description of what you mean?

• What is the easiest way to express your feelings of concern for someone?

• Do people ever confuse these expressions of concern for expressions of romance? How do you handle that?

• Can there be affection without romance?

• Are there ways you express concern for others beyond your family and circle of friends? Is this a kind of love?

• What is the test of a true friendship?

• Is it necessary to test a friendship?

• What are the most important qualities of a friendship?

• What are some dangers to a friendship?

• What's the cause of insincerity? How can we counteract it?

• Why is insincerity a problem? How is sincerity helpful in friendships? In a group?

STORIES AND THOUGHTS FROM SPIRITUAL TRADITIONS

Hinduism

Love expects no reward. Love knows no fear. Love Divine gives – does not demand. Love thinks no evil; imputes no motive. To love is to share and serve.

– Swami Sivananda

One would incur great sin even seeing those who are not distressed at the suffering of a friend.

– Ramcaritmanas

View your own Everest-like pain as nothing more than a grain of dust, while to minuscule problems of a friend as being like a mountain.

– Ramcaritmanas

Buddhism

Love is wishing happiness for living beings. Boundless love is wishing ultimate happiness for infinite living beings, without expecting anything in return.

Hatred is not overcome through hatred, but through love alone.

Love for All

One day the Buddha came upon a group of children who had caught a crab and begun to torture it. The children squealed as one boy ripped off the crab's claws and then its legs, one by one. The Buddha asked the children, "Would it hurt you if someone ripped off your legs?" "Yes," they replied. And the Buddha asked, "Doesn't the crab feel pain just like you? Not only does the crab suffer, but its family members also suffer when the crab feels pain. Think this over carefully." As the children reflected and began to regret their actions, the villagers gathered to hear the Buddha's teaching: "Every living being wants happiness and safety. All living creatures—large and small, two-legged and four-legged, swimmers or flyers—all have the right to live. Therefore let us harm no living being. Let us protect life. Just as a mother protects her only child even at the risk of her own life, so should we too, with open hearts, protect all living beings from harm. Day and night—whether sitting, standing, walking, or lying down—let us be full of love, surrounded by love on all sides. Let us dwell in love always."

Zen Buddhism

Isshin (one-heart) means to throw oneself wholly into the action without any other thought at all.

Christianity

"Let love be genuine; hold fast to what is good."
                                                    – *Bible, Romans 12:9*

"So faith, hope, love abide, these three;
  but the greatest of these is love."   – *Bible, I Corinthians 13:13*

"You shall not commit adultery."   – *Bible, Exodus 20:14*

"And above all things, put on love, which binds
  everything together in perfect harmony."   – *Bible, Colossians 3:14*

"This is my commandment, that you love one
  another as I have loved you."   – *Bible, John 15:12*

Islam

The Nightingale's Excuse

The nightingale made his excuses first.

His pleading notes described the lover's thirst,

And through the crowd hushed silence spread as he

Descanted on love's scope and mystery.

'The secrets of all love are known to me,'

He crooned. 'Throughout the darkest night my song

Resounds, and to my retinue belong

The sweet notes of the melancholy lute,

The plaintive wailing of the lovesick flute;

When love speaks in the should my voice replies

In accents plangent as the ocean's sighs.

The man who hears this song spurns reason's rule;

Grey wisdom is content to be love's fool.

My love is for the rose; I bow to her;

From her dear presence I could never stir.

If she should disappear the nightingale

Would lose his reason and his song would fail,

And though my grief is one that no bird knows,

One being understands my heart—the rose.

I am so drowned in love that I can find

No thought of my existence in my mind.

Her worship is sufficient life for me;

The quest for her is my reality

(And nightingales are not robust or strong;

The path to find the Simorgh* is too long).

My love is here; the journey you propose

Cannot beguile me from my life—the rose.

It is for me she flowers; what greater bliss

Could life provide me—anywhere—than this?

Her buds are mine; she blossoms in my sight—

How could I leave her for a single night?'

The hoopoe answered him: 'Dear
  nightingale,
This superficial love which makes you
  quail
Is only for the outward show of things.
Renounce delusion and prepare your
  wings
For our great quest; sharp thorns defend
  the rose
And beauty such as hers too quickly goes.

True love will see such empty transience
For what it is—a fleeting turbulence
That fills your sleepless nights with grief
  and blame—
Forget the rose's blush and blush for
  shame!
Each spring she laughs, not for you, as
  you say,
But at you—and has faded in a day.'
  *Simorgh is God

– *The Conference of the Birds p 35–37*

By Him in whose hand my soul is! ye shall by no means enter paradise
until ye believe, and ye shall by no means believe until ye love one another.
– *Selections from Mishkat-ul-masabi [444] p 99*
Abu-Hurayrah, MU: AB: TI

Shall I tell you of a thing which when ye do, ye will love one another?
Extend greetings among yourselves.
– *Selections from Mishkat-ul-masabi [445] p 99*
Abu-Hurayrah, MU

Allah's Messenger said: 'None of you has faith unless he loves for his brother
what he loves for himself.'
The love of Allah and His Prophet Muhammad necessarily leads to the love of
His Creation. When we have truly cast our gaze from material rewards and
turned to Him, then our hearts will turn naturally to love of our fellow man.
Love of this kind is not simply a matter of treating another as we would have
him treat us, but of genuine empathy which goes beyond concern for our own
lot.

– *The Essential Teachings of Islam p 3*
4: Hadith (Bukhari) 2:6

Chinese

"Is Goodness indeed so far away? If we really wanted Goodness,
we should find that it was at our very side."
– *Confucius*

"One who has accumulated moral power will certainly also possess eloquence;
but he who has eloquence does not necessarily possess moral power."
– *Confucius*

"When soul and body are in the bond of love, they can be kept together. By concentration on the breath it is brought to perfect elasticity, and one becomes as a babe."
                                                                — *Lao Tzu*

> *The flowery branch of the wild cherry*
> *How swiftly it flies back!*
> *It is not that I do not love you;*
> *But your house is far away.*

The Master said, "He did not really love her. Had he done so, he would not have worried about the distance."   — *The Analects, Book IX*

Jan Jung asked about Goodness. The Master said, "Behave when away from home as though you were in the presence of an important guest. Deal with the common people as though you were officiating at an important sacrifice. Do not do to others what you would not like yourself. Jan Jung said, this is a saying I shall put into practice.   - *The Analects, Book XII*

Judaism

More Love

   Rabbi Pinhas and his disciples reflected on the advice of the Baal Shem in regard to dealing with difficult people. He said that when it is clear that someone dislikes you and wants to do you harm it is necessary to encourage your spirit to love them more. This is the only way that you can make a difference in the relationship. If love and unity prevail among people then the Divine Presence and holiness surrounds them. But if a chasm develops between people then the potential holiness falls into the chasm. So if your neighbor is distant from you in spirit you must bring yourself closer to him, to close up the gap between you.

Native American

The Love Flute

   Once there was a young man who was deeply in love with a beautiful young girl, but he was so shy that he could not bring himself to tell her how he felt. In fact, it was easier for him to go into battle against fearsome enemies than to face the girl he loved. He was brave enough to lead in the buffalo hunt, but he did not have the courage to tell the girl how much he loved her.

   Now, there were other young men who were drawn to the beautiful maiden, as well. They waited proud and confident outside her tipi until she emerged, ready to offer her their lovely blankets and to speak to her. The shy young man looked on from a distance, becoming more and more disappointed in himself. He thought about her every minute of the day, and she even filled his dreams at night. Still, he could say nothing.

Each day the beautiful maiden would go to the river to fetch water, and the shy young man would stay to watch her. The other young men gathered, too, whistling or throwing pebbles to attract her attention. She would smile at them as she passed. It seemed so easy for them to talk and laugh with her. "I think she likes us!" one proud young man said to his friends one day.

"She must like them a lot," thought the shy young man, "after all, they speak to her so easily. They manage to say whatever they want. They chat with her each day. She doesn't even notice me."

His love for her remained quiet, but strong. Yet, the young man grew sadder and sadder with each passing day. He cared little about anything as life for him without the beautiful girl was so empty. One morning, he set out away from the camp, moving aimlessly up the mountainside. Out of sadness and frustration, he shot an arrow high into the sky without aim.

To his surprise, the arrow did not arc downward, but continued to fly far and high in the sky. The young man followed it and managed to keep pace with it throughout the entire day. Finally, at dusk, the arrow curved earthward and fell next to a clear stream. The next morning, the young man sent another arrow flying. He followed it throughout the day until it once again landed near a clear stream. He did the same for four days, sensing that unseen powers were helping him and leading him to something wonderful.

On the fourth evening, he found himself at the edge of a wood. He was tired after his pursuit of the arrow and he lay down to rest. He could not say whether what happened next was real or a dream. He heard the leaves rustling nearby, and the sound of voices whispering around him. "You tell him," said the first. "No, you," a second voice replied. At that moment, two large Elk Men with towering antlers emerged and stood over him.

One bent toward the shy young man saying, "Here is something for you." He held a beautiful flute which next, he put to his lips and played. "You see how lovely its music is? It is made of cedar which grows where winds blow. The woodpecker made these holes for playing. All the other birds and animals helped to make it as well, and we have put our voices inside it. When you play it, you will hear our voices in your songs. The music you make with it will sing to the heart of the girl you love. It will tell her of your love."

Suddenly, there was a flash from a mirror carried by one of the Elk Men, and the young man was blinded. As he tried to regain his eyesight, he saw two bull elks running into the trees. He picked up the flute which had been left behind, and holding it he felt as if something had changed. He blew into the flute and birds all around him joined in his song.

For four days, he made his way back to the camp. He played the flute as he walked and made music with the songs of the birds and sounds of the animals. His songs carried throughout the forest and gave pleasure to all the creatures there.

On the fourth evening, he entered the camp playing his lovely flute. The light breeze carried his songs through the camp and straight to the heart of the beautiful girl he loved so dearly. She knew his music was meant for her. It called to her and she left her tipi to find the young man. When she came upon him, she sat down close to him and listened to the music of his flute. It told her more than words could ever say. "I love you," it sang, over and over.

PROVERBS AND MAXIMS

Love is like a butterfly; it goes where it pleases, and it pleases where it goes.
— *William Penn*

Love without friendship is like a shadow without sun.
— *Japanese Proverb*

Friendship is the best present you can give. — *William Penn*

It is good to love many things, for therein lies the true strength, and whosoever loves much, performs much, and can accomplish much, and what is done in love is well done.
— *Vincent Van Gogh*

"Amor omnia vincit."
(Love conquers all.)

HEROES AND HEROINES

THOMAS ANTHONY DOOLEY (1927–1961)

Born in St. Louis, Missouri, he developed an early interest in serving people and chose medicine as the best way to accomplish his goals. He joined the Navy in 1953 and within a year was involved in providing medical relief for Vietnamese refugees. He established a medical mission in northern Laos in 1956, followed by hospitals in Cambodia and Vietnam. In 1957 he established Medico, an international medical aid mission. He wrote several books that reflect on the needs of people and the connections between morality and the human spirit: *Deliver Us from Evil, Edge of Tomorrow* and *The Night They Burned the Mountain.* He is an excellent example of the many physicians who chose a service of love over a lucrative medical practice. His early death cut short a promising life of commitment to the world's health needs.

ELIZABETH FRY (1780–1845)

She was born in Norwich, England into a family that had belonged to the Society of Friends (Quakers) for generations. Her father, John Gurney, was a successful banker. When Elizabeth was seventeen, she became a Plain Quaker, dressing in plain clothes and giving up all personal adornments. She married a London merchant named Joseph Fry, also a Quaker. In 1813 she learned about the terrible conditions in Newgate Prison. Located in one of the oldest and worst parts of London, it housed over 400 women and 50 children in four small rooms with no beds, no heat, no toilets, no ventilation and no light. She visited the prison, encouraged the women, and started talking to prison officials and lawmakers about improving the conditions. Because the behavior of the prisoners improved when they were treated better, her ideas spread throughout England. Soon rulers from France, Denmark, Holland and Prussia asked for her advice. Her actions of love and kindness reformed the prisons and the laws of much of Europe.

ANNE MANSFIELD SULLIVAN MACY (1866–1936)

Born in Feeding Hills, Massachusetts near Springfield, Anne was the teacher who became the lifelong friend of Helen Keller. Anne married John Macy in 1905. In 1887, at age 21, she was chosen as the teacher of Helen Keller who was without sight and hearing and unable to speak. Where others had failed, Anne Sullivan didn't give up and with as much love as skill and teaching techniques taught Helen to speak. Her patient and courageous love enabled the frightened and underdeveloped Helen to become a mature and successful person. In time, they were close friends and companions.

JOHN MUIR (1838–1914)

Born in Dunbar, Scotland, of rather harsh and pious parents, he moved to America with his family in 1849. They settled near Portage, Wisconsin. Forbidden to waste daylight hours on reading, John was granted permission to get up early. So, he invented a machine that would dump him out of bed at one o'clock in the morning. He studied science and medicine at the University of Wisconsin but gave it up for jobs that challenged his inventive skills. In 1867, he changed his mind again, giving up his own inventions "to study the inventions of God." He began walking across America, keeping a journal of scientific and personal observations as well as pencil sketches. His writings as a naturalist and an explorer are still important to conservationists. His love of nature and his exploration of Yosemite Valley were instrumental in establishing Yosemite National Park.

ST. FRANCIS OF ASSISI (1182–1226)

Born in Assisi, Italy, and given the name Giovanni, he was called Francis by his father, a successful cloth merchant who raised him to appreciate luxury. When he was twenty, Francis was taken a prisoner of war and underwent several religious experiences. As a result, he renounced any claim to his father's wealth or name and entered a life of poverty and service to others. He thought the church needed to return to the original message of Christ, which was to love all people and all creatures. A number of young men were inspired by his example and asked to join his way of life. In 1209, they presented their ideas for a new religious community to the Pope, and the order of Franciscans was formed. By 1223, he was spending more and more time in prayer and meditation, leaving the decisions about the order to others. His last two years were spent in constant pain and near blindness. He was canonized as a saint two years after his death.

JANE GOODALL (1934–)

Born in London, England she moved with parents and sister to Bournemouth on the English coast. While she did well in her studies, Jane much preferred learning about animals and insects, and playing outside. The love of all creatures began when she was two years old after her mother gave her a stuffed toy chimpanzee. Once, she was caught sleeping with earthworms under her pillow and, another time, waited for five hours for a hen to lay an egg. Unhappy with life as a secretary, she left for Nairobi, Africa in search of the famed paleontologist Louis F. B. Leakey. She won Leakey's trust and admiration. The scientific world was amazed when Leakey sent this twenty-four year old woman, who had worked only as a waitress and a secretary, into the wilds to study chimpanzees. Her ability to observe, to collect and analyze scientific data, and write reports as an animal activist earned her worldwide acclaim as an ethologist. Her love for animals is seen in this statement about the chimpanzees: "Surely we must speak for them—for they cannot speak for themselves."

PUT LOVE INTO ACTION

- Offer a word of encouragement to someone who is struggling with some work.

- Speak with someone you don't know very well.

- Say what you mean nicely; without sarcasm.

- Continue with your random acts of kindness.

- Tell your parents and other family members that you love them.

- Listen to someone who seems to be having a bad day.

- Compliment someone about something.

- Thank your parents for something they've done.

- Write a letter of thanks or appreciation to someone.

- Show a love for nature by making a birdfeeder to help feed the birds until spring.

- Show your sincere friendship with a smile—all day long.

- Smile and warmly shake hands with new people you meet.

COMMUNITY SERVICE IDEAS

- Plan and carry out a "Love in a Baggie" project: gallon bags filled with toiletry items and decorated with a happy message, then delivered to the homeless.

- Make and deliver care packages for AIDS patients: decorated hand-carry bags filled with toiletry items, food, and books.

- Help make Kiddie Sacks (bags of goodies) for underprivileged kids.

- Volunteer at a Hospital for Children: plan recreational activities, read books, do crafts, etc.

- Volunteer at a shelter, assisting in the care of infants and toddlers.

- Develop a big brother/ big sister program within your school. Schedule fun activities throughout the year for big/little brother/sister teams. End the year with a big/little brother/sister school olympics and award ceremony.

- Broadcast the message of love, friendship, and sincerity to your community by making signs and banners to hang up in a public place, or hand out bookmarks your class made from the pattern on page 112 to customers at a local bookstore or post office.

- Promote friendship across the ocean by establishing a pen pal connection with a student your age on another continent.

BOOKS ON LOVE

A *Mother for Choco*. Keiko Kasza. New York: Putnam, 1992.

Girl Who Loved Wild Horses. Paul Goble. Scarsdale: Broadway Press, 1978.

Porcelain Man. Richard Kennedy. Boston: Little, Brown, 1976.

The Stupids. Harry Allard. Boston: Houghton Mifflin, 1978.

Wolf's Chicken Stew. Keiko Kasza. New York: Putnam, 1987.

The Book of Virtues. William J. Bennett, ed. New York: Simon and Schuster, 1993.

 "Damon and Pythias" – p. 306

 "The House By the Side of the Road" – p. 305

 "How Robin Hood Met Little John" – p. 308

 "Little Girls Wiser than Men" – p. 318

 "The Selfish Giant" – p. 292

 "The Velveteen Rabbit" – p. 275

A Call to Character. Colin Greer and Herbert Kohl, eds. New York: Harper Collins Publishers, 1995.

 "Frankenstein" – p. 434

 "The Glove and the Lions" – p. 428

 "More Adventures of the Great Brain" – p. 420

The Moral Compass. William J. Bennett, ed. New York: Simon and Schuster, 1995.

 "What Men Live By" – p. 788

Wisdom

SUPPORTIVE VALUES

Knowledge • Insight

DEFINITIONS

Deep understanding; the ability to choose and act with sound judgment.

Wisdom is a trait we admire as we age, and a quality we acquire as we become more aware of our surroundings, our relationships, and ourselves. Often we think it is a characteristic obtained through experience, yet we all know of the wisdom which we often read in our students' work or observe in their interactions with each other, regardless of their age and despite their seeming lack of experience and knowledge.

Knowledge and **insight** are used in defining wisdom, and ideally education is a vehicle for obtaining wisdom. Through the experiences which we offer our students academically, socially, musically, artistically, physically, and spiritually - knowledge and insight are natural results. Yet we are cautioned by the wise, "You must not hold a thought just because many other people hold it, nor because it has been believed for centuries, nor because it is written in some book which men think sacred; you must think of the matter for yourself, and judge for yourself whether it is reasonable." (J. Krishnamurti) This is essentially the process of critical thinking which we prize so highly and strive to develop in our students. Gibran says it another way, that the wise educator "does not bid you enter the house of his wisdom, but rather leads you to the threshold of your own mind."

PURPOSE

The purpose of highlighting wisdom as a value which we honor is twofold. We acknowledge wisdom as a virtue which we recognize in others and strive to obtain for ourselves, so that we may better serve others. "Study then, but study first that which will most help you to help others. Work patiently at your studies, not that men may think you wise, not even that you may have the happiness of being wise, but because only the wise man can be wisely helpful." (J. Krishnamurti) We are all capable of making wise decisions when we take the time to look at the various choices and the consequences of those choices. Much of what we refer to as wisdom is an awareness of what is happening in and around us. If we develop awareness, we are taking our first steps toward wisdom. In becoming knowledgeable and understanding, we can make wiser choices regarding our relationships and our actions as they affect the world around us.

Wisdom

Day One:
In your own words, write a definition of wisdom as you would normally define it. Then look at the definitions on page 119, and compare with your own definition.

Day Two:
Think of all the people you know personally who impress you as being very wise. Make a list of ten "wise people" of your acquaintance. Beside each person's name write one or two adjectives that describes a trait that caused you to include them on the list.

Day Three:
Do you think modern technology is helping people of today gain wisdom or could it possibly encourage people to be less concerned with seeking wisdom? Explain your answer.

Day Four:
Write a journal entry about an act or a decision on the part of one of your teachers or school administrators that you feel demonstrated wisdom.

Day Five:
What connection to age does wisdom have? Are there more elderly wise people or more young wise people? Explain your answer.

Day Six:
Why and how should we respect the wisdom of others? How does the wisdom of adults benefit kids on issues of 1) health 2) education 3) safety 4) quality of life?

Day Seven:
Imagine what a world without wisdom would be like. Discuss your ideas with your classmates. Would you like to live in such a world? Why or why not?

Day Eight:
Newspaper columns and journal entries are often labeled "wit and wisdom." How are these two words alike and different? Fold a sheet of paper in half, vertically. Label one side "wit" and the other "wisdom." Write five quotes, proverbs or maxims on each side that illustrates the label.

Day Nine:
In a total class setting, share and discuss "wit and wisdom" lists compiled yesterday.

Day Ten:
Plan and create a long wall mural or banner featuring stylized writing and painting and colorful illustrations to display the best of the proverbs, quotes and maxims. Base selections for inclusion on the class's interpretation of true wit and wisdom.

Day Eleven:
Prepare a chalk talk or illustrated mini-lecture on the meaning of the following statement for people of your age as they plan for their future. "People become wise gradually and at different rates, one decision and one action at a time."

Day Twelve:
Research the life of a famous person whose actions reflect true wisdom. Make a time line of the person's life to show how wisdom increased during the person's life span.

Day Thirteen:
Pretend you have been given responsibility for explaining the concept of wisdom to a younger person. Write a comprehensive explanation of what it is and why it is an important value, using simple and non-complex sentences to be easily understood by the younger person.

Day Fourteen:
Remember a time when you shared some of your wisdom with another person. Write or draw about the experience in your journal.

Day Fifteen:
Do some research in the library to find a mythical figure which represents wisdom. Some ideas are: unicorns, magicians, wizards, and dragons. Remember to also look into Greek and Roman mythologies! Prepare a shoebox diorama to show the wisdom of this character. Display for the whole class to see.

Day Sixteen:
Discuss the different mythological characters that are represented by the reports. In a group setting, think about why storytellers choose these wise characters as the focus of their dramas.

Day Seventeen:
Increase your own personal wisdom. Go to the library and select the encyclopedia which holds the information about the letter that also begins your name (e.g., Judy Thompson—J or T). Turn to a random page and read about the topic explained there.

Day Eighteen:
Share your wisdom. Exchange the wisdom you gained yesterday with a partner.

Day Nineteen:
Work in small groups to create a brand new proverb, slogan or maxim related to the search for wisdom. Devise a "wise" and creative way to share it with the total group.

Day Twenty:
Reflect on the importance of developing respect for wisdom as a desirable value at an early age and on ways young people can begin to establish goals and habits that lead to wisdom.

WISDOM IN OTHER LANGUAGES

Chinese	*zhi*	wisdom; knowledge; cleverness; prudence
French	*la sagesse*	a characteristic of a person showing itself in right judgement, aware and informed decisions and actions; behavior of an obedient, tranquil child; an ideal of life based upon a moral or philosophical doctrine
German	*weisheit*	to have wisdom, knowledge, learning
Hawaiian	*na'auao*	learned, enlightened, intelligent, wise
Japanese	*chi*	the God entered into a person and one keeps talking
Korean	*hyun myung*	wise and bright, acumen, discernment
Latin	*sapientia*	from Gothic "-witi" (wit) (having one's wits together)
Spanish	*sabidura*	wisdom, knowledge, learning
Tagalog	*karunungan*	being wise in conduct and words; knowledge and good judgement based on experiences

Character Education Year 1 Grades 6–12

DISCUSSION QUESTIONS

- How would you explain the purpose of school to someone your age who has never had the opportunity of going to school? Would they like to go to school or feel sorry for you?

- What are the most important things you are supposed to learn in school?

- What would you like to learn?

- What are the ways knowledge will help you as you grow older?

- How does knowledge increase your appreciation and understanding of other people? Other cultures?

- Are there important things that you learn outside the classroom? Without books?

- Should people be given the choice of going to school or not? At what age?

- When should you have the choice of what subjects you take? Why? What would you take? Why?

- How would you describe an educated person?

- What should a person your age know?

- What is the difference between being smart (intelligent) and being wise?

- What motivates a person to learn? What motivates you?

- Has anyone learned anything from you?

- Is understanding more important than knowledge? Why or why not?

- How do you plan to use the knowledge you've gained in school?

STORIES AND THOUGHTS FROM SPIRITUAL TRADITIONS

Hinduism

The childish go after outward pleasures;
They walk into the net of widespread death.
But the wise, knowing immortality.
Do not seek permanent (eternal) among the unstable things in this world.

– Upanishads

He who knows little speaks much.
He is wise who speaks little, but his words have great value.　　*– Tradition*

The wise realize that the Absolute (God) is everywhere, but
cannot be perceived nor grasped, is without beginning, eyes,
ears, hands, or feet, is eternal, with multiple forms, all pervasive,
subtle, undiminished, and the source of all that is.　　*– Upanishads*

"I" and "mine," "you" and "yours" is nothing but illusion,
The feelings that have kept all souls in confusion.
The objects of the senses, as far as the mind can go,
All is but illusion, truly you should know.　　*– Ramcaritmanas*

The person who possesses the innocence of childhood,
vigor of youth, and wisdom of old age is capable of
truly knowing the Divine.　　*– Tradition*

In the land of the blind, the one-eyed is king.　　*– Tradition*

Buddhism

Wisdom is the insight that uproots all delusions. Wisdom is more than intelligence, more than the common sense to act appropriately in life situations. Wisdom means seeing directly into the true nature of things.

Due to ignorance, we mistakenly suppose things exist as they appear. Deceived by the illusion of an independent self, we create many unwholesome actions. Finally, with the sword of wisdom, we cut through this illusion and free the mind from ordinary appearances. Manjushri represents the power of wisdom of all the Buddhas. Deftly wielding his sword of wisdom, he eliminates all the delusions from the root. With practice we, too, can awake from the slumber of ignorance and see things "as they are."

　　　　　　　Character Education Year 1 Grades 6–12　123

Wisdom is the antidote to unknowing. As babes, we are ignorant of everything, concerned only with fulfilling our own desires. As children, controlled by our emotions, we ignore the needs of others. As adults, our vision gets clouded by desires and we become attached to intoxicants, sense pleasures, and worldly pursuits. Ignorant of the consequences, we create negative deeds out of attachment to loved ones and aversion to others. After some time, we grow old. Our health declines and our beauty fades. Our hair grows white, our teeth fall out, and our energy ebbs, but still we cling to our bad habits and possessions. After death, due to our negative deeds, we spin out of control into unfortunate states of rebirth.

The past is gone, the future has not come. The present moment is the most important moment of our life. Therefore, now is the time to learn all we can, purify our mind, do good deeds, and develop the wisdom that understands the true nature of things.

Sitting under the bodhi tree, Shakyamuni developed the wisdom to see things "as they are." Through his own meditation experience, he discovered the Four Noble Truths: that living beings experience dissatisfaction and suffering, that suffering is caused by desire, that suffering can come to an end, that the way to eliminate suffering is to follow the Noble Eightfold Path: right understanding, right intention, right speech, right action, right livelihood, right effort, right mindfulness, and right concentration. This path directly leads to nirvana: liberation from all sufferings, from birth, and from death.

Zen Buddhism

When a man sees a dream, everything in it is taken as real, but on awakening there is nothing there at all. Delusive thought is like a dream, and when regarded from the waking standpoint it has never been there. Living beings are confused and take the delusion for reality.

Christianity

"Happy are those who find wisdom for they also find life."
– Bible, Proverbs 8:32-35

"Wisdom builds her house, but folly with her own hands tears it down."
– Bible, Proverbs 14:1

"Everyone who hears these words of mine and does them will
be like a wise man who built his house upon a rock."   *– Bible, Matthew 7:24*

Solomon the Wise King

The Lord appeared to King Solomon in a dream one night and told him to ask for anything he wanted, and it would be given to him!

Solomon replied, "You were wonderfully kind to my father, David, because he was honest and true and faithful to you, and obeyed your commands. And you have continued your kindness to him by giving him a son to succeed him. O Lord my God, now you have made me the king instead of my father, but I am as a little child who doesn't know his way around. And here I am among your chosen people, a nation so great that there are almost too many people to count! Give me an understanding mind so that I can govern your people well and know the difference between what is right and what is wrong. For who by himself is able to carry such a heavy responsibility?"

The Lord was pleased with his reply and was glad that Solomon had asked for wisdom. So he replied, "Because you have asked for wisdom in governing my people, and haven't asked for a long life or riches for yourself, or the defeat of your enemies—yes, I will give you what you have asked for! I will give you a wiser mind than anyone else has ever had or ever will have! And I will also give you what you didn't ask for—riches and honor! And no one in all the world will be as rich and famous as you for the rest of your life! And I will give you a long life if you follow me and obey my laws as your father David did.

Then Solomon woke up and realized it had been a dream. He went to Jerusalem and went into the Tabernacle. And as he stood before the Ark of the Covenant of the Lord, he sacrificed burnt offerings and peace offerings. Then he invited all of his officials to a great banquet.

Soon afterwards two young prostitutes came to King Solomon to have an argument settled.

"Sir," one of them began, "we live in the same house, just the two of us, and recently, I had a baby. When it was three days old, this woman's baby was born too. But her baby died during the night when she rolled over on it in her sleep and smothered it. Then she got up in the night and took my son from beside me while I was asleep, and laid her dead child in my arms and took mine to sleep beside her. And in the morning when I tried to feed my baby it was dead! But when it became light outside, I saw that it wasn't my son at all."

Then the other woman interrupted, "It certainly was her son, and the living child is mine."

"No," the first woman said, "the dead one is yours and the living one is mine." And so they argued back and forth before the king.

Then King Solomon said, "Let's get the facts straight: both of you claim the living child, and each says that the dead child belongs to the other. All right, bring me a sword." So a sword was brought to the king. Then he said, "Divide the living child in two and give half to each of these women!"

Then the woman who really was the mother of the child, and who loved him very much, cried out, "Oh, no, sir! Give her the child—don't kill him!"

But the other woman said, "All right, it will be neither yours nor mine; divide it between us!"

Then the king said, "Give the baby to the woman who wants him to live, for she is the mother!"

Word of King Solomon's decision spread quickly throughout the entire nation, and all the people were awed as they realized the great wisdom God had given him.

Bible – 1 Kings 3:5-28

Islam

The Valley of Insight into Mystery

The next broad valley which the traveler sees
Brings insight into hidden mysteries;
Here every pilgrim takes a different way,
And different spirits different rules obey.
Each soul and body has its level here
And climbs or falls within its proper sphere—
There are so many roads, and each is fit
For that one pilgrim who must follow it.
How could a spider or a tiny ant
Tread the same path as some huge elephant?
Each pilgrim's progress is commensurate
With his specific qualities and state
(No matter how it strives, what gnat could fly
As swiftly as the winds that scour the sky?).
Our pathways differ—no bird ever knows
The secret route by which another goes.
Our insight comes to us by different signs;
One prays in mosques and one in idols' shrines—
But when Truth's sunlight clears the upper air,
Each pilgrim sees that he is welcomed there.
His essence will shine forth; the worlds that seemed
A furnace will be sweeter than he dreamed.
He will perceive the marrow, not the skin—
The Self will disappear; then, form within
The heart of all he sees, there will ascend
The longed-for face of the immortal Friend.
A hundred thousand secrets will be known
When that unveiled, surpassing face is shown—
A hundred thousand men must faint and fail
Till one shall draw aside the secrets' veil—
Perfected, of rare courage he must be
To dive through that immense, uncharted sea.

If you discern such hidden truths and feel

Joy flood your life, do not relax your zeal;

Though thirst is quenched, though you are bathed in bliss

Beyond all possible hypothesis,

Though you should reach the throne of God, implore

Him still unceasingly: "Is there yet more?"

Now let the sea of gnosis drown your mind,

Or dust and death are all that you will find.

If you ignore our quest and idly sleep,

You will not glimpse the Friend; rise now and weep.

And if you cannot find His beauty here,

Seek out Truth's mysteries and persevere!

But shame on you, you fool! Bow down your head;

Accept a donkey's bridle and be led!

– The Conference of the Birds p 179-80

He grants wisdom to whom He pleases and whosoever is granted wisdom is rich indeed. But none will grasp the Message except men of understanding.

All knowledge belongs to Allah. Everything we learn, from the first recognition of our own self as an individual to the recognition of Allah, is granted by Him. Knowledge comes to us when and how Allah wills. . . .

– The Essential Teachings of Islam p 148
230: The Cow (Baqara) 2:269

High above all is Allah, the King, the Truth. Do not be in a rush with the Qur'an before its revelation to you is complete, but say: 'O my Lord, advance me in Knowledge.'

Just as the unfolding of the Qur'an to the Apostle and his people was a gradual process, so it is for any individual who approaches it. True knowledge can never be grasped all at once by anyone other than Allah. So we must be patient, allowing the meaning and purpose of the Qur'an to unveil itself according to our own capacity and Allah's Will. We must be humble in the realization that our knowledge can never be complete; there is no end to what we can learn from it, the complete Revelation and final Revelation of Allah.

– The Essential Teachings of Islam p 148
231: Mystic Letters TH (TA HA) 20:114

The Messenger of Allah said: 'The seeking of knowledge is obligatory upon every Muslim.'

> *— The Essential Teachings of Islam p 151*
> *235: Hadith*
> *Ibn.-I-Majah 224*

Chinese

"To learn and at due times to repeat what one has learnt, is that not after all a pleasure? That friends should come to one from afar, is this not after all delightful? To remain unsoured even though one's merits are unrecognized by others, is that not after all what is expected of a gentleman?" *— Confucius*

"He who learns but does not think, is lost. He who thinks but does not learn is in great danger. *— Confucius*

"Let one's intelligence comprehend every quarter; but let his knowledge cease, that he may understand." *— Lao Tzu*

Hawaii

The Owl Who Saved the Boy

Na'ilima was playing a string game while waiting for her brother to finish fishing in the bay below her. She watched a school of silvery fish come near him and wondered if he saw them. He threw his net at the right moment and pulled the catch in. She was proud of her brother who was a skilled fisherman even though he was just a young boy.

While she was watching her brother, she didn't see a canoe enter the bay. The men paddled toward the beach where her brother was pulling in his catch. They took away his net and threw the fish back into the ocean. They surrounded him, tied him up and put him into the canoe and paddled away. Na'ilima was so worried about her brother she began to cry. Why have they taken my brother? He must have broken a kapu since one of the men was a priest. He could die if he broke a kapu. She followed the canoe along a cliff trail overlooking the sea and saw that they took her brother to a temple. They were going to kill her young brother!

She started praying to her family guardian god, the owl. "Please save my brother, he did not know that he was breaking a kapu. Please save him." She repeated her prayer over and over. Soon an owl appeared and perched near Na'ilima as if to say he had heard her prayer and was going to help. He flew off toward the temple.

At dusk, the owl perched on a wall of the temple and saw that the guards were asleep. He flew over and with his powerful beak he began to pull on the cords that bound the boy. The boy's hands were now free so he could untie his feet. Once freed, he quietly climbed the temple wall, although he was aching and sore. He started to run toward the path that would take him to his sister, but the owl struck him with his strong wings. The boy understood that the owl didn't want him to run and didn't want him to face the direction he wanted to go. As frustrated as he was the boy understood that for some reason he was being forced to walk backward by the owl, whom he knew to be his guardian, so he obeyed. Whenever he tried to turn and run, the owl would strike him with his wings until he turned backward and walked.

Finally, they came to the rock where Na'ilima sat praying and crying with worry. She quickly embraced her brother then heard voices in the distance coming toward them. "It must be those who captured you," she whispered. "Hide in this hole under the rock." The men with torches arrived and asked her if she had seen anyone. "No one has come this way," she replied.

"Here are his tracks!" yelled one of the guards. "He went this way!" exclaimed another who held his torch over a footprint in the soft dirt. They all hurried off, following the tracks that the boy had made back to the temple. The brother and sister ran quietly off together and were soon safe at home.

India

Something That is Everything

One day Emperor Akar was galloping back to Agra when he saw a crowd under a banyan tree. He heard that a very wise sage sat there. Akbar returned to the place disguised as a commoner, met the sage, and asked him to pass on some wisdom.

"Give me something that is everything and I will give you wisdom," said the sage. Akbar was puzzled. Back in the palace, Akbar told his friend Birbal what puzzled him. "My lord, I have plenty of that thing!" said Birbal.

Both Akbar and Birbal, disguised, proceeded to meet the sage. Akbar was surprised that Birbal was not carrying anything with him. "Have you brought something that is everything?" the sage asked Akbar. Akbar looked at Birbal. Birbal picked up a handful of dust. "Here it is. Man or monument, prince or pauper, sage or fool, plant or animal, all become dust. This is something that is everything," said Birbal.

The sage looked at Akbar and said, "You wanted wisdom from me. One who has this man as his friend needs no wisdom from me."

Ukrainia

When to Relax and When to Act

In the northern frontier of Ukraine there is a peaceful village named Luvar. The people work in their fields and live happily. The fields yield them enough; the river gives them plenty of water; the neighbors are ready to help one another.

But, as in any other village in the world, there are always some villagers who are more active than the others and a few who are less active than the others. But there was one man in the village Luvar who did not fall into either category, for he just did not work! He was Nikhailo. A piece of his land was tilled by another farmer who supplied him with three meals a day. So far as a cup of tea was concerned, Nikhailo knew how to earn it. He would just step into the house of one of his neighbors and say, "It is pretty cold today isn't it?"

"It is, Nikhailo, it is. It is always very cold for one who does not wish to move out of one's shelter. But perhaps you would like to warm yourself with a cup of tea," the neighbor would observe courteously. And, of course, Nikhailo would have his cup of tea.

Now, it so happened that Nikhailo's uncle died leaving him a piece of vineyard. "You have to work very little, but you will get plenty," the uncle told Nikhailo before closing his eyes forever. Nikhailo very smartly agreed to do the necessary "very little."

But that was all he did. He did not even go to see the field.

A vixen (a she-fox) and her cubs lived in a comfortable hole in the field. The cubs played and frolicked about freely all over the field, for nobody ever visited it. But as the spring came, Nikhailo finally walked over to the field. He stood on a small mound of earth and surveyed the field and yawned and said, "Tomorrow I must come and uproot all the grass!" Then he went away.

The fox cubs who had seen and listened to him with bated breath, ran to their mother and said, "A man is coming to denude the field of all the grass. He will find us out and probably kill us. What to do?"

"Which man are you speaking of? Nikhailo? Don't you worry, my children. Play on as usual," said the mother fox and she dozed off!

Indeed, there was no sign of Nikhailo the next day or the day after!

But he was there once again after three months. He took position on the mound and said again, "I see, the grass has become very tall! Tomorrow I will come and cut it all!" Then he went away.

The cubs reported the matter to the mother, with less anxiety this time. The mother nodded and said, "Never mind!"

Another three months passed. Nikhailo appeared there once again. By then the grass had dried up. "I see," he said, "I think I should fetch a little fire and burn the dry grass!"

He left, and this time the fox cubs did not even feel it necessary to report the man's observation to their mother. But the mother fox shouted at them, saying, "Come on, children, we leave at once!" The children obeyed their mother. They had just reached the riverbank when they saw the field on fire!

"To put fire to something is so easy that even Nikhailo would do it!" the vixen explained to her cubs.

Judaism

The Scholars

Moshe Efraim, a grandson of the Baal Shem, was a very dedicated student and eventually became a great scholar which made him depart from the teachings of his grandfather. His grandfather would often go walking with him, although, Efraim was somewhat reluctant about these walks since he begrudged the time away from his studies.

Once, they met a man walking towards them who had come from another city. The Baal Shem asked him about one of the people from his city to which the man replied, "He is a great scholar." The Baal Shem responded, "I envy him his scholarship, but what am I to do? I must serve my maker, I have no time for studying." From this moment on, Efraim followed his grandfather's teachings and the hasidic way of life with all his heart.

Chinese

Chen and the Great Bronze Bell

Long, long ago in China there lived a very wise man named Chen. He was not only clever, but he was also fair, and was admired and respected by all. People who sought justice would come to Chen, seeking his advice and accepting his decisions.

One night there was a great robbery committed in the district in which Chen lived. The people were outraged and angry. Several suspects were rounded up quickly, but no one could be certain as to who the thief really was. All of them were questioned for hours and still the townspeople could not decide who the guilty one was. It was decided that they all should be taken to Chen. Certainly he would be able to solve the mystery.

Chen listened to each person's story, but instead of asking them questions he simply said, "There is a great bronze bell which hangs in the temple to the East. It will be able to tell us who the robber is."

Chen sent several men to carry the beautifully polished bell from the temple to the town for it was extremely large and heavy. When the men finally arrived with it, Chen ordered them to construct a cloth canopy over it. They made it from a large square of cotton which they

Character Education Year 1 Grades 6–12

mounted on four poles. Once they were done, Chen sent the men away. He set firepots to burn all around the great bell. The fires burned through the night and when they finally died away, Chen carefully removed the poles and let the cotton canopy fall gently so that it completely covered the great bell like a blanket.

The next day, people from all around came to see the bell and to witness the trial. They knew that Chen would identify the thief, and they wanted to see how he would do it. There were so many people that there was scarcely any room for the suspects. When everyone was assembled, Chen stood before them and said, "This old bronze bell has powers beyond my own. It can determine guilt and innocence with speed and certainty. Ten thousand innocent people may rub it and it will not make a sound. But should one thief touch it, the bell will sound for people to hear for miles around!" Then Chen knelt before the bell and made a prayer over it. He turned to the suspects and said, "Each one of you shall reach under the cloth and rub the bell. It will sound when the guilty one touches it."

One by one, each suspect approached the bell and slipped one hand under the cloth to rub it. As each one turned away from the bell without having made it ring, the crown let out a sigh. When the last one had passed the test and no sound was heard the crowd became restless. The bell had failed! But Chen moved forward and clasped the arm of the last suspect. "Here is our thief!" Chen exclaimed.

The accused man turned to the crowd and said, "That's ridiculous! The bell made no sound when I touched it. I am as innocent as all the others."

It was then that Chen instructed some men to remove the cover from the bell. People could see that the once shiny bronze bell was now blackened with soot. There were shiny streaks where the suspects hands had rubbed the soot away.

"This bell has truly great powers," declared Chen. "Indeed, it made no sound when innocent people rubbed it. Neither did it ring when the thief put his hand under the cover. But alas, the thief was afraid to touch it lest he make the bell sound out his guilt. Thus, only the hands of the thief remain clean and free of soot." All eyes fell to the blackened hands of the innocent suspects, then to the clean hands of the guilty man.

All agreed that Chen possessed great power and wisdom indeed.

Japanese

The Wise Old Woman

Long ago, in a village in the hills of Japan, there lived an old woman and her son, a farmer. They lived a simple, but good life. But the village was ruled by a cruel young lord who imposed many strict laws over the villagers. One day he issued a proclamation. "Anyone over seventy years of age is no longer useful to the village," were the lord's harsh words. "Any person who reaches that age is to be taken into the mountains and left to die."

When the young farmer's mother reached her seventieth birthday he was saddened by what he had to do according to the lord's rule. He could not bear to take his mother far from their home and leave her alone to die. His heart broke with the thought of carrying out the lord's command. But his mother knew of his duty. Placing her hand gently on that of her son, she said, "The time has come for you to take me into the mountains."

So, sadly, the next morning, the son carried his beloved mother on his back along the steep mountain path. The trees grew dense and the air chilly as he made his way higher and higher. The mother snapped twigs from the trees and dropped them as he walked, saying, "I am marking the path for your safe return, my son."

The son could bear the heartbreak no longer. "I will not leave you alone in the mountains, mother," he said. "I am taking you back to our home and I will never leave you."

With that, protected by the shadows of the night, he carried his mother all the way back down the mountain path to their home. He dug a secret room beneath the kitchen where his mother spent her days. She was so well hidden that no one knew of their secret.

A few years had passed when one day there was a great commotion as some of the great Lord Higa's warriors descended on the village in a whirlwind. They rode up to the young lord's estate and shouted for him to hear. "This is a warning from the mighty Lord Higa," they cried. "In three days time he will sweep through your village and conquer it!"

The young lord was cowardly and implored of them, "Please spare my life. I will do anything you ask!"

"Lord Higa has no pity for you or your little village," one of the warriors replied. "He does, however, have great respect for a clever mind. If you solve the three impossible tasks written on this scroll, you and your village will be spared."

The young lord caught the scroll as the warriors turned and thundered off. Nervously, he unrolled the scroll to reveal the first impossible task. "The first task is to make a coil of rope out of ashes," it read. "Secondly," the young lord continued to read, "you must run a thread all the way through a crooked log. And thirdly, you must make a drum that plays without being hit."

The young lord quickly called the very wisest people of the village to his palace. He commanded them to solve the impossible tasks, but try as they might they could not come up with the solutions. They begged the gods for help, but there was no response.

In a panic, they sought the cunning badger who lived in the forest and who had outsmarted people many a time. "Please, help us!" they implored. But even the badger was not clever enough to solve the impossible tasks.

The young lord was furious when the wisest people of the village returned to him without answers. "You are nothing but fools!" he cried, and swiftly threw them into prison. He was now desperate to find the answers and offered a bag of gold to anyone who could help him. The news of the lord's plight and the threat to the village spread quickly.

The young farmer spoke to his mother of the impossible tasks. "This is terrible," he said. "In no time at all our village will be conquered by yet another cruel lord."

His mother remained silent for a few moments as she thought. Then she told her son to bring her a coil of rope, a crooked log, and a small drum. When he returned with the objects, she began by soaking the coil of rope in salt water, then leaving it to dry completely. Then, she lit one end of it with a match. They watched as the flame traveled through the rope all the way to the other end. The young farmer was amazed that although the burning rope had turned to blackened ashes, it did not crumble, but instead, held its shape. "There is your rope of ash," she said.

Next, she picked up the gnarled and crooked log. She dabbed a bit of honey on one end of it, and at the other she placed an ant to which she had tied a silk thread. The ant, eager to find the honey, made its way through the twists and turns of the log, all the while pulling the silk thread. When it finally arrived at the honey the mother said, "The second task is done."

Lastly, she took the small drum and opened up the skin on one side. She placed a bumblebee inside and resealed the drum. The bee flew about within the drum, trying to escape. It hit against the skin repeatedly, making the drum play without being beaten. "And now the last task has been completed," the mother said calmly.

The young farmer ran to his lord's palace and presented the solutions to him. The lord was amazed and could not believe that the farmer had been clever enough to complete the tasks. "Surely someone must have helped you. Who is it that had the wisdom to do this?" the lord asked sternly.

The farmer confessed that in fact, it was his wise old mother who had solved the problems. He admitted that he had kept her hidden for several years as he could not bear to leave her in the mountains on her seventieth birthday. "She is the one who has saved us from the threat of Lord Higa," the farmer said. He waited for the lord to unleash his fury for disobeying the law.

But the young lord sat quietly, looking at the poor farmer. Finally, in a low voice he said, "I have been wrong. Our old people are of great value to us. I should never have sent them into the mountains to die, and it will be done no longer. From now on, they shall be treated with respect, and their wisdom will be treasured."

The next day, the young farmer marched with the lord's warriors to Lord Higa's castle. Upon their arrival, he presented the rope of ash, the threaded log, and the drum that played without being beaten to the mighty Lord Higa. A slow smile spread across Lord Higa's face. "So," he said thoughtfully, "you have solved the three impossible tasks. There must be much wisdom in your little village." Looking at the young farmer he said, "Go back to your lord and tell him that your people deserve to live in peace."

Never again was the young lord cruel or unfair to his people. The young farmer and his mother lived happily for the rest of their long lives.

PROVERBS AND MAXIMS

> To understand life is to understand ourselves and that is both the beginning and the end of education. — *J. Krishnamurti*

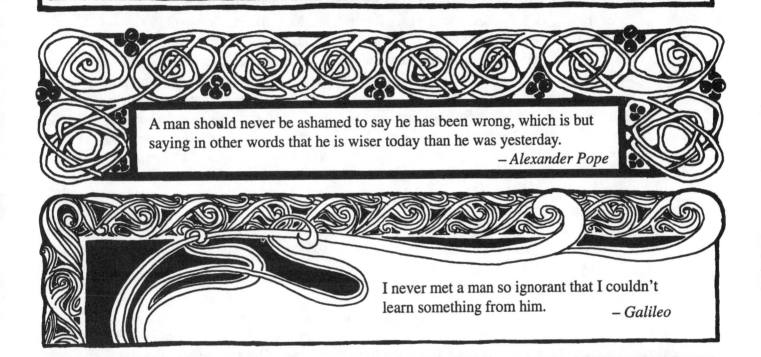

A man should never be ashamed to say he has been wrong, which is but saying in other words that he is wiser today than he was yesterday.
— *Alexander Pope*

I never met a man so ignorant that I couldn't learn something from him.
— *Galileo*

A wise man is one who knows the difference between good, sound reasons, and reasons that sound good.
— *Alexander Pope*

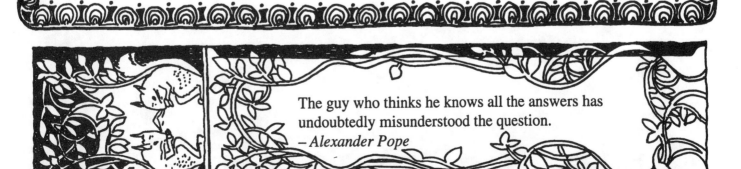

The guy who thinks he knows all the answers has undoubtedly misunderstood the question.
— *Alexander Pope*

HEROES AND HEROINES

DOROTHY DAY (1897–1980)

Born in Brooklyn, New York, she was the daughter of a newspaper sports writer who traveled widely with his family. Living in San Francisco and Chicago and never feeling close to family or friends, Dorothy developed a love for literature and writing. College life and a core of radical friends gave her a foundation of new social, cultural, and political ideas. Bored with college life, she moved to New York City and joined the Bohemian culture of Greenwich Village. World War I brought an end to this life, and she worked for a short time as a nurse. She drifted for several years as a writer and after the birth of a daughter immersed herself in religious literature and theology. She was baptized into the Roman Catholic Church and was faithful to the Church for the rest of her life. In 1932, she discovered a connection between her concern for justice and her religious faith and, with Peter Maurin, founded a newspaper that would communicate their views—the Catholic Worker. For the next fifty years she was a voice of wisdom for Catholic reform, the labor movement, the civil rights movement, the peace movement, and "liberation theology."

ALBERT EINSTEIN (1879–1955)

Born in Ulm, Germany, he grew up in and obtained his early education in Munich. Not exactly a child prodigy, he still wasn't speaking fluently at age nine. However, by age twelve he discovered Euclidean geometry and by age sixteen had mastered differential and integral calculus. He found school intolerable and was expelled because of his negative attitude. He failed entrance examinations to the Federal Institute of Technology in Zurich because of his lack of knowledge in other than scientific disciplines. There are only a handful of people who share the honor of initiating a revolution in scientific thought: Copernicus, Newton and Einstein are three. His insights into the natural world forever changed the world view of physicists and philosophers, and his achievements literally revolutionized physics. He is best known for his theory of relativity.

PLATO (428–347 B.C.E.)

Born in Athens, Greece of aristocratic parents, he lived his whole life in Athens. Little is known of his early years, but we know that he eventually traveled to Sicily, southern Italy and perhaps to Egypt. He was given the finest education Athens could offer, and he was a close associate of Socrates. When Socrates was unjustly executed, Plato turned in disgust from Athenian politics and focused his attention on philosophy. He founded the famous Academy, one of the great philosophical schools of antiquity, that existed for nearly a thousand years and had an enormous impact on the development of Western philosophy. Some scholars have suggested that the Academy may have been a type of religious brotherhood. His philosophical system attracted many followers in the centuries after his death and some of his ideas emerged in the movement of Neoplatonism that became a rival of early Christianity.

SOCRATES (469–399 B.C.E.)

Born in Athens, Greece, the son of a stone mason and sculptor, he learned his father's trade and practiced it for several years before turning to intellectual interests. He was also involved in three military campaigns for Athens. Though he was rather short in stature, he earned a reputation for great prowess and endurance in battle. There are accounts of his entering a kind of trance while in deep thought and he was observed offering prayers to the sunrise. Thus, he was an interesting mixture of warrior for justice, religious mystic, impromptu speaker, and teacher of philosophy and logic; his Socratic method of argumentation became famous. He was brought to trial on trumped-up charges of impiety and corrupting the youth of Athens, and he was forced to take the poison hemlock. Without founding a specific philosophical system, school, sect, or organization, and though he didn't profess any wisdom, his influence on people and on philosophy is immeasurable.

SOLOMON (ca. 980–925 B.C.E.)

Born in Jerusalem, he was the youngest son of David and Bathsheba. He inherited a huge kingdom and ruled with immense power and splendor. Both history and legend have attributed to him great wisdom. He became famous as a wise and fair judge and he is credited with writing three books of the Old Testament—Proverbs, Ecclesiastes and the Song of Solomon. He also possessed good diplomatic skills and was able to build important liaisons with other rulers. His forty-year reign was one of peace. He was responsible for the fortification of several towns in his kingdom and the construction of a series of elaborate structures in Jerusalem, including luxurious palaces, a wall around the city, and a magnificent temple on Mount Moriah. He sponsored industrial enterprises, built a great fleet of ships, and carried on extensive trade with other nations. To have "the wisdom of Solomon" has been the goal of many people.

PUT WISDOM INTO ACTION

- Discuss with your parents the wisdom of a particular character in a movie or video you've seen.

- Take some time to wonder about yourself, people, the world around you.

- Write about your wondering.

- Always be in the process of reading a good book.

- Choose an older friend and ask them a question about life.

- Find something difficult to understand and research it.

- Make a list of things you know which would show your wisdom. Imagine how your wisdom will grow as you do!

- Share your wisdom in a subject when you see a classmate struggling.

- Call or write a grandparent or elderly neighbor and ask them to share their wisdom with you.

COMMUNITY SERVICE IDEAS

- Become pen pals with residents of a retirement home; exchange ideas and learn from their wisdom.

- Collect books for a local or national literacy program.

- Volunteer to read to children in the hospital.

- Organize a Back-to-School Drive to collect school supplies for underprivileged children.

- Volunteer as a guide at a local museum.

- Invite a person of wisdom to speak to your class. Ask him or her to share some wisdom. (Examples of people to invite: local mayor, grandparent of a class member, local chief of police, etc.)

- Increase your family's wisdom. Make-up an "Interesting Fact" quiz. Do some research to develop 20 interesting questions (be sure to record the answers) and take them home for your family.

BOOKS ON WISDOM

Fortune-tellers. Lloyd Alexander. New York: Dutton Children's Books, 1992.

Helga's Dowry: a troll love story. Tomi de Paola. New York: Harcourt Brace Jovanovich, 1977.

It Could be Worse: a yiddish folktale. Margo Zemach. New York: Farrar, Strauss & Giroux, 1976.

A Penny a Look: an old story. Harve Zemach. New York: Farrar, Strauss & Giroux, 1971.

Wretched Stone. Chris Van Allsburg. Boston: Houghton Mifflin, 1991.

The Book of Virtues. William J. Bennett, ed. New York: Simon and Schuster, 1993.

    "Boy Wanted" – p. 78

    "The Frogs and the Well" – p. 52

    "George Washington's Rules of Civility" – p. 74

    "Vaulting Ambition, Which O'erleaps Itself" – p. 85

A 2nd Helping of Chicken Soup for the Soul. Jack Canfield and Mark Victor Hansen. Deerfield Beach: Health Communications, Inc., 1995.

    "Napoleon and the Furrier" – p. 302

    "A Sense of a Goose" – p. 307

    "Wisdom" – p. 301

A 3rd Serving of Chicken Soup for the Soul. Jack Canfield and Mark Victor Hansen. Deerfield Beach: Health Communications, Inc., 1996

    "The Secrets of Heaven and Hell" – p. 320

    "The Secret of Life" – p. 319

    "The Wisdom of One Word" – p. 316

Health

SUPPORTIVE VALUES

Holistic Living • Serenity

DEFINITIONS

The condition of being sound in body, mind and spirit.

With all of the recent research concerning the mind-body connection, we are slowly becoming aware of how much our mental health affects our physical and spiritual health, and vice versa. This is knowledge which Asians have applied for centuries, and the Greeks and Romans espoused as well. The entire movement in holistic health is based on this idea, that our mind-body-spirit are interconnected, interdependent, and not separate, individual entities.

The partner values of **holistic living** and **serenity** emphasize the need to fully understand the importance of living a complete or whole life balancing physical, mental, social-emotional, and spiritual needs. "Utter calm and unruffled repose" are the poetic phrases which define serenity—the hopeful result of a healthy life.

PURPOSE

One goal of teachers is to encourage students to become "well-rounded." This requires a commitment to providing an environment where students develop morally and spiritually, intellectually and physically, creatively and with an appreciation for the arts and for cultural diversity. There also is a desire to instill within them a sense of social responsibility. Health is a necessary component in the achievement of these goals. All of the basics in physical health—eat right, sleep enough, exercise regularly—are a good place to start. This month we will focus on how to live holistically and with serenity in our fragmented, often stressful workaday worlds. Darwin remarked, "If I had my life to live over again, I would have made a rule to read some poetry and listen to some music at least once a week; for perhaps the parts of my brain now atrophied would have thus been kept active through use. The loss of these tastes is a loss of happiness, and may possibly be injurious to the intellect, and more probably to the moral character, by enfeebling the emotional part of our nature."

Health

Day One:
Using the definitions on page 141, discuss the meaning of health.

Day Two:
Compare and contrast the meanings of emotional health, mental health, and physical health. Which is the most important to you? Write a short essay explaining why.

Day Three:
What value does the society in which we live place on health? Look in newspapers and magazines to see ways in which health is portrayed in the media. Does society view health in a "healthy" way? Discuss in small groups.

Day Four:
Rate your own health. Make a list of what you typically eat in a twenty-four hour period. Also make a list of how much physical activity you do each day. On a scale of one to ten, how healthy do you think you are? (If you use drugs, alcohol or cigarettes you must subtract 2 points from your total!)

Day Five:
Do some research to find out what the five food groups are and how much exercise a person of your age should do each day. Based on the list you wrote yesterday and the facts you discovered today, re-rate your health.

Day Six:
Unless you scored a ten, you can improve your health! Devise a realistic plan to become more healthy. Write yourself a letter of encouragement to stick to your plan. Give the letter to your teacher. He or she will give it back to you later to serve as a "self-reminder" of health!

Day Seven:
Divide the class into several small groups. How many different types of exercise can your group think of? The group with the largest number of original ideas wins!

Day Eight:
Use the discussion questions on page 144 to explore your thinking about health.

Day Nine:
Read one of the stories on pages 145-146. Discuss the type of health the story is based on.

Day Ten:
Is there a spiritual dimension to health? Write a journal entry to record your thoughts.

Day Eleven:
Choose and color a bookmark on page 147. Keep it in your health textbook to remind you to practice good health.

Day Twelve:
Drugs are a big threat to your health. Plan with a partner how you would say no to someone who was offering you drugs.

Day Thirteen:
Do you know what smoking cigarettes or marijuana can do to your lungs? Find some pictures of lungs who have been blackened by smoke.

Day Fourteen:
Organize a fund-raiser to encourage healthy living in your community. Gather pledges from friends or family and skip rope or shoot baskets for donations. (i.e. 10 cents for each basket shot within a two minute time limit.) Donate the money to pay medical expenses for kids without health insurance.

Day Fifteen:
Good hygiene is key to good health. Collect deodorant, toothpaste, toothbrushes, soap and other toiletries to be given to a local shelter.

Day Sixteen:
Choose one of the heroes or heroines of good health on pages 148-149. Write a short story about what the world would be like today without that person's contribution to health.

Day Seventeen:
Plan a healthy meal for your family. Make a menu and list of ingredients that you will need. Take your plan home and prepare this meal if you are able.

Day Eighteen:
Water is one of the most important elements of good health. Try to drink the prescribed eight glasses today.

Day Nineteen:
Open the letter you wrote to yourself earlier in the month encouraging good health. Have you stuck to your plan? If not, recommit yourself to follow through. If so, congratulations—keep it up!

Day Twenty:
Reflect on what you have learned about health this month. Decide to embrace a life-long commitment to health.

HEALTH IN OTHER LANGUAGES

Chinese	*jian*	strong, robust, vigorous; to strengthen; to invigorate
	shen	body
French	*la santé*	condition of a person whose organism is working well; equilibrium of the personality and control of intellectual capacity
German	*gesundheit*	soundness of health, wholesomeness, salubrity
Hawaiian	*olakino maika'i*	good state of health (ola means "life, health, well-being," kino means "body, person, individual" and maika'i means "goodness, righteousness")
Japanese	*shinshin*	a balance of "mind and body"
Korean	*kun kang*	sound and vigor, well-being
Latin	*valetudo*	from Gothic "hal" (whole) (health is "wholeness"; related to "wholesome")
Spanish	*salud*	health, well-being, welfare
Tagalog	*kalusugan*	being well or not sick; freedom from sickness

DISCUSSION QUESTIONS

- Why do people become sick when they are worried? When they're afraid? When they're bored?

- What other emotions affect you physically?

- What is the most important part of one's self to keep healthy—body, mind, or spirit? Why?

- Is it difficult to maintain the proper balance? Why? What works for you? What part do you try to improve first? Why?

- Do you need other people to feel better or can you rely on yourself? Does faith help?

- What is the connection between physical health and mental health?

- What is the relationship between exercise and one's outlook on life?

- How much does stress play in your own state of health?

- How do you cope with stress?

- Does stress always come from outside sources or do we create it for ourselves?

- Can you give an example of a serene person?

- Why are they serene? Is it possible for everyone?

STORIES AND THOUGHTS FROM SPIRITUAL TRADITIONS

Hinduism

The key to realization and liberation is a healthy body.　　*– Charaka Samhita*

A soft stomach [i.e., no gastric problems], warm feet [i.e., good circulation],
and a cool head [i.e., no fever, anger, etc], lead to long life.　　*– Tradition*

As you eat, so you think.　　*– Tradition*

Food that is prepared or given with love is filled with
spiritual nutrition, food that is not should not be eaten.　　*– Tradition*

Buddhism

Buddha Shakyamuni taught that there are 84,000 different emotional afflictions—arising from desire, hatred, and ignorance—which affect beings adversely and produce 84,000 different physical disorders. Illness is common to all living beings, and ultimately the way to eliminate it is to purify the mind.

The Buddha is likened to a doctor, the spiritual teachings are like medicine that cures the afflictions, and spiritual friends are like the nurses who help administer the medicine.

Moderation is the key to physical well-being. Avoid eating too much, talking too much, or thinking too much. A healthy person is one who achieves physical and mental balance.

The physical, intellectual, and spiritual well-being of each person are integrally related. Curing the body alone, without paying attention to a person's mental and spiritual health, is insufficient. The human organism is a dynamic whole. When the humors of the body—wind, bile, and phlegm—are in balance, we enjoy health and happiness. When the humors get out of balance, we are vulnerable to various afflictions. A calm and positive state of mind is essential for maintaining optimum health. Ailments can also be treated on a karmic level, by creating good deeds such as saving lives, practicing generosity, reciting mantras, and practicing meditation. Imagining ourselves surrounded and filled with the light of compassion also helps prevent illness and injury.

Zen Buddhism

We often compare the state of our minds to that of our stomachs. When we are in good health, we forget that our stomachs even exist. But, as soon as we have a stomachache, we are

　　　　Character Education Year 1 Grades 6–12　**145**

continually conscious of the pain there. This is because we don't pay attention to our bodies until we become ill. Only then, for the first time, we become conscious of the part that is ailing. In the same way as long as we live in peace and good health, we are not even conscious of our own selves.

Christianity

"For we are the temple of the Living God."   — *Bible, II Corinthians 6:16*

"The fear (knowledge) of the Lord prolongs life,
but the years of the wicked will be cut short."   — *Bible, Proverbs 10:27*

"Pleasant words are like a honeycomb, sweetness
to the soul and health to the body."   — *Bible, Proverbs 16:24*

Islam

Who so wakes up in the morning in the full security of his heart, and his body free from harm, having also his day's food, it is as though the world, all of it, is driven to him.

— *Selections from Mishkat-ul-masabi [127] p 32*
'Ubaydu'llah b. Mihsan, TI

Chinese

The Master said, He who will not worry about what is far off will soon find something worse than worry close at hand. Those who are capable of spending a whole day together without ever once discussing questions of right or wrong, but who content themselves with performing petty acts of clemency, are indeed difficult to lead into the Way.

— *The Analects, Book XV*

Judaism

The Immersion Bath

The Baal Shem was very devoted to completely immersing himself in rivers or streams or a large bath. He believed that this practice was more beneficial to the body than abusing it by fasting for long periods or by hurting the flesh in other ways. These abusive practices were often done by those who thought they would make one more holy. The Baal Shem said that these practices only served to weaken " . . . the strength you need for devotions and teaching, the bath of immersion heightens this strength."

PROVERBS AND MAXIMS

He who has health has hope and he who has hope has everything.
— Arabian Proverb

The first wealth is health. — *Emerson*

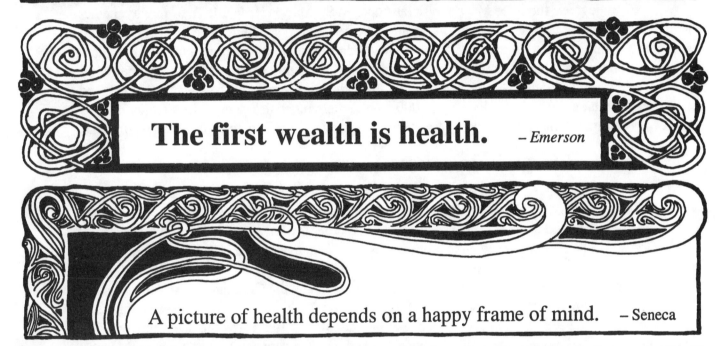

A picture of health depends on a happy frame of mind. — *Seneca*

"Pars sanitatis velle sanare fuit."

(Part of the cure is the desire to be cured.)

—Seneca

A wise man should consider that health is
the greatest of human blessings.
— Hippocrates

HEROES AND HEROINES

THE MAYO BROTHERS—WILLIAM JAMES MAYO (1861–1939) AND CHARLES HORACE MAYO (1865–1939)

Born the sons of an English medical doctor, William was born in Le Sereur, Minnesota and Charles was born in Rochester, Minnesota. Will and Charlie grew up surrounded by medicine and during the early evolvement of surgery. In 1889, a year after they had both received their medical degrees, the three Mayo physicians opened St. Mary's Hospital. Their nearby medical offices became a cornerstone in American medicine –the Mayo Clinic. The brothers were physicians, scientists and humanitarians. They didn't hesitate in welcoming the unfortunate to their clinics and thirty percent of their patients were pleasantly surprised to receive their bills marked "Paid in Full." No one was charged more than ten percent of their annual income and every dollar collected on bills over $1,000 went to help other sick people. As successful as they became as physicians, they were even more successful as brothers and as humanitarians.

FLORENCE NIGHTINGALE (1820–1910)

Born in Florence, Italy of wealthy parents, she easily could have slipped into a life of luxury and pleasure. However, she possessed a strong spirit that inspired her to seek independence and a spiritual conscience that moved her toward a profession and service to God. In 1844, Florence decided to work in hospitals and, against her parents demands that "ladies" did not become nurses, she found some private nursing and a few months in a German school and hospital. She volunteered for service in the Crimean War in Turkey and struggled with the barbaric conditions of a field hospital. She created order and cleanliness, and mostly through the improvement of sanitary conditions, decreased the death rate by two-thirds. She led the reform of military hospitals and medical care and founded a school for the training of nurses. Her "Notes on Hospitals," published in 1859, gave detailed directions for the design of civilian hospitals.

ROBERT ALLAN NORDYKE (1919–1997)

Born in Woodland, California, a small town in the Sacramento Valley, he was reared in a large family of seven children and modest means. He graduated from the University of California at Berkeley with a major in English literature, political science, and public speaking. Following four years of military service during World War II, he entered medical school at U.C. San Francisco working as a trash-hauler to pay expenses. Bob and his wife, Ellie, were married in 1950 and, after a shoestring trip around the world, they settled in Los Angeles for his residency in medicine. It wasn't long before they moved to Honolulu where Bob became a pioneer in nuclear medicine, computerized medicine, and medical informatics. He is renowned as a medical researcher, publisher, and administrator. Beyond all his accomplishments in medicine, he will be remembered as a dedicated family man and a compassionate, caring human being.

LOUIS PASTEUR (1822–1895)

Born in the small town of Dole, France, the son of a tanner, Louis graduated from college at age eighteen with a degree in the arts. His doctorate was focused on the obscure science of crystallography which would have a decisive influence on his career. He was famous at age twenty-six when he demonstrated the phenomenon of optical isomers. In 1854, he became Professor of Chemistry and Dean of Sciences at the University of Lille and began his work on fermentation. He quickly designed experiments that eliminated the process of fermentation, thus developing the techniques of "pasteurization." This was not only helpful in the preserving of wine, beer, and milk, but also led to the reduction of infection in hospital operating rooms. Other scientific triumphs for the world of health included his work on germ theory and the development of vaccines. Sterilization of surgical instruments, steaming of bandages, controlling anthrax and a vaccine for rabies are just some of the results of his work.

JONAS EDWARD SALK (1914–1995)

Born in New York City, he entered the College of the City of New York at age sixteen to study law. He changed to medicine and graduated from the College of Medicine of New York University in 1939. In 1942, he went to the University of Michigan, where he developed an influenza vaccine. From there he moved to the University of Pittsburgh as associate professor of bacteriology and continued his research on a polio vaccine. By 1950, he had developed a vaccine against all three types of polio, and in 1955, after five years of testing, it was determined safe for the public. By the time he died, polio had disappeared from the United States. In 1963, he opened the Salk Institute for Biological Studies in San Diego, where he studied problems related to the body's rejection of organ transplants.

ALBERT SCHWEITZER (1875–1965)

Born in Kaysenberg, in upper Alsace (which then belonged to Germany), the son of a Lutheran minister, Albert moved with his family to Gunsbach, Germany when he was young. Surrounded by music and intelligent conversation, he quickly developed interests in several areas. He became proficient at the piano and organ and was playing for his father's Sunday services at age 9. When he began college, he made the decision to absorb all he could with his mind, especially of the things he loved, until age thirty, at which time he would devote himself to the service of humanity. He first earned a doctorate in philosophy and then a doctorate in theology. He then focused on music and organ building, becoming an expert in both. In 1905, at age thirty, he began to study medicine and announced that he was preparing for mission work in Africa. Graduating in 1912, he left soon after for French Equatorial Africa and started a hospital in Lambarene, Gebon. His work soon became famous around the world. World War I interrupted his work for seven years, and upon returning to Lamborene, Albert found his hospital in ruins; so he rebuilt it. Though he had written books in philosophy, theology and musicology, his greatest accomplishment was in service to the poor. His humanitarian work earned him the Nobel Peace Prize. He was still working at age ninety on his monumental three-volume work *Philosophy of Civilization*.

PUT HEALTH INTO ACTION

- Try to avoid "junk" food and snack on fruit and vegetables instead.

- Get some exercise every day.

- Get enough sleep to have energy throughout the day.

- Notice something beautiful in nature every day.

- Change a negative thought into a positive thought.

- Be aware of how great it is to feel healthy and strive to stay healthy.

- Eat balanced meals.

- Do something everyday to exercise the mind; read, do crossword puzzles, engage in thoughtful discussions.

- Do something everyday to improve a relationship.

- Do something everyday to exercise the spirit; meditate, pray, read spiritual literature, do something for others.

- Spend a few minutes each day in complete relaxation.

COMMUNITY SERVICE IDEAS

- Volunteer with the Poison Control Center Booth.

- Help stencil storm drains with warnings about toxic materials.

- Volunteer at a Health Fair; help organize one. (Arthritis Foundation)

- Volunteer at a local park for some weeding and cleaning.

- Assist with fund raising and special events at the American Cancer Society.

- Aid in the health of nature by weeding gardens on your school grounds or in a nearby park.

- Organize a "Run for Your Health" race. Hold the race for members of your community. Collect a nominal entry fee and donate the proceeds to an organization dedicated to health.

- Remind people in your community to be in charge of their physical, emotional, and mental health through creating signs to hang-up in public places.

BOOKS ON HEALTH

Gilgamesh, the King. Ludmila Zeman. Plattsburgh: Tundra Books, 1992.

Green Man. Gail Haley. New York: Scribner, 1979.

A 3rd Serving of Chicken Soup for the Soul. Jack Canfield and Mark Victor Hansen. Deerfield Beach: Health Communications, Inc., 1996
  "The Beauty Remains; The Pain Passes" – p. 275
  "We Never Told Him He Couldn't Do It" – p. 259

A 4th Course of Chicken Soup for the Soul. Jack Canfield "etal." Deerfield Beach: Health Communications, Inc., 1997
  "State of Mind" – p. 326
  "The Trouble Tree" – p. 310

A 5th Portion of Chicken Soup for the Soul. Jack Canfield and Mark Victor Hansen. Deerfield Beach: Health Communications, Inc., 1996
  "Consider This" – p. 301
  "The Best Time of My Life" – p. 344

The Moral Compass. William J. Bennett, ed. New York: Simon and Schuster, 1995.
  "The Prayer" – p. 751

Humor

SUPPORTIVE VALUES

Joy • Enthusiasm

DEFINITIONS

The ability to see, express or enjoy the ridiculous, unexpected or unusual.

When speaking of character traits or values we admire in a person, a sense of humor is often near the top of the list. Simply defined, **humor** is to discover, express, or appreciate the ludicrous, unexpected, or the absurd. Basically what we are referring to in regard to humor is anything which amuses us or makes us laugh and takes the edge off the seriousness in our sometimes too serious lives. The two kinds of humor which we want to focus on this month are best described by the following quotes: "A little nonsense now and then is relished by the wisest men," and "Happy is the person who can laugh at himself. He will never cease to be amused." We will focus on humor that allows us to enjoy the nonsense in life and encourage the ability to laugh at ourselves.

Our partner values of **joy** and **enthusiasm** refer to the attitudes which we have toward the way we live our lives. Joy is defined as a state of happiness or delight and enthusiasm is a feeling of strong excitement.

PURPOSE

We are seeking to highlight humor, which enriches us by bringing joy and thus enthusiasm to our everyday lives. From a joyful and enthusiastic perspective we tend to treat others in a positive way, kindly and respectfully. We are all aware of humor which is unkind and disrespectful. It is, therefore, important that we recall our values of respect, kindness, and sincerity in our use of humor as teachers and also in the kind of humor we allow our students to use. Usually joy and enthusiasm are natural attributes of children, but the frequent, pseudo-sophisticated use of the word "boring" by many of our students speaks of neither joy nor enthusiasm. Joy can be found in the simplest of things, and an understanding of this hopefully can breed an enthusiasm for life and all it has to offer. This month we want to help instill an understanding of kind and respectful humor and the importance of joy and enthusiasm in our lives.

Day One: Discuss the meaning of humor using the definitions on page 153.	**Day Two:** Make flashcards and work with a partner to practice using the words from other languages that have the same meaning as humor. See page 155.	**Day Three:** Go to the library and find a joke book. Memorize one to share with your family tonight.	**Day Four:** Write a journal entry about telling the joke last night. Was it fun? How did your audience react?	**Day Five:** Create a "Joker of the Week" award to give to a student who best represented the value of humor this week. Continue this award each week for the entire month.
Day Six: Why is it important to be able to laugh at yourself in certain situations? Draw a cartoon strip of an incident when you were able to laugh at yourself.	**Day Seven:** Joy helps start the day right. As a class, create a humorous and joyful morning announcement to share with the school over the P.A. system or through a school assembly. (Ideas: play music, tell a joke, perform a funny short skit, etc.)	**Day Eight:** Use the discussion questions on page 156 to conduct small group discussions.	**Day Nine:** Write a funny original story. Make a book by compiling the stories of all your classmates. Make copies for each student.	**Day Ten:** Choose and decorate a bookmark from page 164. Mail the bookmark to a friend or relative who you don't see very often.
Day Eleven: Choose an activity from page 167 for the whole class to do today.	**Day Twelve:** Share the most simple and basic gift of joy. Try to smile at every member of your class at least one time today.	**Day Thirteen:** Study the heroes and heroines of humor on pages 165–166. Write a short journal entry about the humorous person you would most like to emulate.	**Day Fourteen:** Plan a community service activity to share the value of humor. (See page 168 for ideas)	**Day Fifteen:** Put your community service plan into action!
Day Sixteen: Imagine an alien spaceship lands in your classroom. These aliens come from a planet where there is no laughter. How would you describe the benefits of laughter to these visitors?	**Day Seventeen:** Read one of the stories on pages 157-163. What does the story teach us about humor? Discuss your thoughts with your classmates.	**Day Eighteen:** Plan to give one person joy today. Pick a person you know and then plan an action that will give that person joy. (i.e. Do the dishes for your mom tonight; visit an elderly neighbor and tell him or her about your day; or give a small treat to a classmate.)	**Day Nineteen:** Write a journal entry about your plan to give joy. Were you successful? Did giving another person joy also give you joy?	**Day Twenty:** Reflect on what you have learned about humor. Remember to include a sense of humor in your everyday life!

HUMOR IN OTHER LANGUAGES

Chinese	—————	There is no Chinese character for the meaning of humor. There is no concept of humor in the Asian mind.
French	*l'humour*	a form of wit which focuses with drollness or fun upon the ridiculous, absurd, and unusual aspects of reality
German	*humor*	humor
Hawaiian	*ho'o makeaka*	"to cause laughter" (makeaka means "witty, comic, funny, amusing" and ho'o is a causative)
Japanese	*yuumoa*	a way of saying "humor" in Japanese (see Chinese)
Korean	*ik sal*	wise crack, wit
Latin	*facetiae*	from Latin "umor" (body fluid) (Originally our word "humor" came from the Latin word "umor" meaning a body fluid. So it took on the meaning of "disposition" (Latin "ingenium"). If your "humors" were bad, you were in a poor disposition . . . bad mood. Your "humors" determined your "nature" (Latin "natura"). So having a good nature means you are good-humored. If you are good-humored, you are perhaps humorous.)
Spanish	*humor*	humor, wit, mood
Tagalog	*katatawanan*	to have a funny quality; a joke or jest; seeing the funny side of life

DISCUSSION QUESTIONS

• What does it mean to have a sense of humor?

• Why is it healthy to laugh at oneself?

• What is the difference between laughing at someone and laughing with someone?

• How would you describe the phrase "filled with joy"? What would take away this feeling?

• What things have to be present in your life for you to be happy? Are they things or people?

• How does a good sense of humor contribute to a person's health?

• What happens when someone takes themselves too seriously?

• Can you develop a sense of humor? How?

• At what age do you think people give up the attitude of playfulness? Why do they?

• What creates a feeling of "pure joy?"

• What role does enthusiasm play in being happy?

• Can you be happy when you're by yourself?

• How much of your happiness depends on other people?

STORIES AND THOUGHTS FROM SPIRITUAL TRADITIONS

Hinduism

Where there is joy, there is creation. Where there is no joy, there is no creation.
— *Upanishads*

Happiness can only be had by renouncing attachment to the cycle of birth, disease, old age, and death.
— *Hitopadesha*

He who is able to transcend both desire and anger is called a saint and is truly happy.
— *Bhagavad Gita*

The person who knows he is neither body nor mind, but instead the eternal Self, finds the source of true joy and abides there eternally.
— *Upanishads*

Buddhism

Be friendly to all and speak with gentle words. It is easy to love those who are lovable, but difficult to love those who are nasty and gruff. So whether people are rich or poor, educated or uneducated, acquaintances or strangers, the challenge is to be equally friendly and kind to all.

When the great Zen master Nan-chuan died, one of his senior disciples was found standing before the master's coffin roaring with laughter. Another disciple was appalled at this outrageous behavior and scolded him: "Is this the way you show respect to your dear departed teacher? How can you laugh in the face of such a terrible loss?"

The first disciple said, "If you will explain the Buddha's teaching to me, I will stop." The second disciple stood there without saying a word. Lamenting this deplorable state of affairs, the first disciple began sobbing with grief. "Alas, our dear teacher is indeed gone."

Islam

Allah Collects Interest

The effendi urgently needed money but could find no one who could lend him ten dinars. Not knowing what he could do anymore, in the middle of the night he began to implore the All-Merciful: "Allah, All-Merciful, I pray, grant me this favor, give me ten dinars. If you cannot give them to me outright, I would be satisfied even with a loan."

The effendi had not finished his prayer when he heard somebody knocking loudly at the door. He signalled his wife to go to the door. The visitor was the local official governing one hundred families. "Nasreddin," he began, "it is necessary again to repair the mosque. Allah, who protects you in every hour of the day, said that your part for the work is five dinars."

The effendi sighed and said, "Alas, Allah asks very high interest. He has not loaned me anything yet and already he wants to be paid back!"

– The Effendi and the Pregnant Pot p 82-3

Christianity

"A cheerful heart is good medicine."   *– Bible, Proverbs 17:22*

"To make an apt answer is a joy and a word in season, how good it is!"
– Bible, Proverbs 15:25

David Dances Before the Ark

David brought the Ark to the city of David with a great celebration. After the men who were carrying it had gone, David danced before the Lord with all his might. So Israel brought home the Ark of the Lord with much shouting and blowing of trumpets.

But as the procession came into the city, Michal, Saul's daughter, watched from a window and saw King David leaping and dancing before the Lord; and she was filled with contempt for him.

The Ark was placed inside the tent which David had prepared for it; and he sacrificed burnt offerings and peace offerings to the Lord. Then he blessed the people in the name of the Lord of Heaven, and gave a present to everyone—men and women alike. When it was all over, and everyone had gone home, David returned to bless his family.

But Michal came out to meet him and exclaimed in disgust, "How glorious the king of Israel looked today! He exposed himself to the girls along the street like a common pervert!"

David retorted, "I was dancing before the Lord who chose me above your father and his family and who appointed me as a leader of Israel, the people of the Lord! So I am willing to act like a fool in order to show my joy in the Lord. Yes, and I am willing to look more foolish than this . . . "

– Bible, II Samuel 6:12-21

India

The Hunter of Justice

Pramod of our village was working in the city. I must admit that nobody else from our village was employed in the city, and only a few had occasionally visited it.

Pramod walked and talked in a very superior way. He look down on everybody in the village. He spoke of the city as if it was a fairyland!

No doubt, he commanded some respect from the people of his own age. So far as the elders were concerned, they just tolerated him.

But how would the children of the village understand that he had any reason to be proud? Why should Mintu, Rintu, Raghu and Bapi show him any respect?

One day while the children were playing in the village square, Pramod happened to pass by. Now, the children played a game called 'Strike the Stick'. They would set a stick on the sands. Then, from a certain distance, they would throw another stick at it. One who could strike the target at the first throw would gain a point.

It was Mintu's turn to hurl the stick. He hurled it; but suddenly Pramod came between him and the target. Mintu's stick hit Pramod's leg.

"You loafer! I will teach you how to behave!" yelled Pramod. He rushed at Mintu, but Mintu ran away. Pramod tried to catch him, but in vain. Can a bull ever catch a mongoose?

The angry Pramod reported the matter to Mintu's father Ranganath.

I'm sorry, Pramod, I will ask the boy and his friends, not to change the village square into a playground!" said Ranganath.

"That is all right," said Pramod with some disgust, "but what about the mischief your son has already done?"

It is not his mischief, Pramod, it is his mistake. Don't you remember how you and I too used to play the same game?" Ranganath reminded him smiling politely.

But it had no effect on Pramod. "I want justice!" he shouted.

"I see," said Ranganath gravely. "In that case you have to complain to Chowdhury!"

Chowdhury was a highly revered figure in that area. His was the last word on any dispute. People accepted his judgements without any murmur.

Chowdhury lived in an adjoining village. As Pramod headed in that direction, he came face to face with Diwakar.

"Hello, Pramod, why must you walk so fast? What is the matter with you?" asked Diwakar. Pramod gave the reason. But Diwakar smiled and said, "Pramod, must you grow so very angry for such a trifle? Have peace!"

"It is easy to lecture on peace!" shouted Pramod. "I want justice!"

"Very well. Go ahead!" said Diwakar.

Chowdhury was amused at Pramod's complaint, but he did not show that he had taken the complaint lightly. Instead, he said, "You see, such cases are judged by Diwakar of your village. I give my attention to other kinds of cases!"

"But Diwakar only knows how to lecture on peace. He does not understand the need for justice!" complained Pramod.

"You tell him that I want him to do justice in this case," said Chowdhury. But Pramod was not satisfied. He brought Diwakar to Chowdhury. Diwakar promised to do justice.

Back in their village, Diwakar called all the respectable men of the village and placed Pramod's case before them: "Mintu is to blame for his conduct. Pramod should either forgive him or punish him. Pramod is bent on punishing him. What do you say?" he asked.

Mishra, the headmaster of the village school, said, "Mintu has not struck Pramod deliberately. That is why it will not be proper for Pramod to strike Mintu deliberately. He can only throw a stick at Mintu's leg."

"That is correct," agreed all.

"But Mintu may run away. How can I throw a stick at him?" asked Pramod.

"Mintu shall be held by two of us. But see to it that your stick strikes only Mintu, not the others!" cautioned Diwakar.

But it was not necessary to hold Mintu. He stood on his own. Pramod took aim and hurled a stick at his legs, but it missed them. He was given two more chances, but he missed them. Those present could not check their laughter. Pramod felt terribly humiliated. He fled.

"Mintu, if you kept standing today without any fear, what made you run away when Pramod wanted to catch you?" Diwakar asked the boy, giving him a pat on the back.

"I did not know how he would have punished me then. Now, before all my guardians, he could not have done anything he liked. What is more, my father assured me that Uncle Pramod was his playmate and that Uncle Pramod could never hit his target!"

There was an uproarious laughter. Pramod left for the city the same day.

Judaism

These next two brief tales deal with Humor's partner value, joy, as it is expressed in Hasidism. Martin Buber explains, "The core of Hasidic teachings is the concept of a life of fervor, of exalted joy." He continues, " . . . this joy must not be the goal toward which you strive . . . personal joy will rise up when you want nothing but the joy of God—nothing but joy in itself."

The Dance of the Hasidim

At a special Jewish festival, Baal Shem and his disciples were having a party and enjoying the wine, which kept coming from the cellar, and the dancing. After several hours of this, Baal Shem's wife said to him, "If this party continues we will have no wine left for any of the festivals for the rest of the year." The Baal Shem laughed and agreed that this was so. He told his wife to tell them to stop. She went to the big room where they were enjoying themselves dancing in a circle, a blazing ring of blue fire weaved around them. She then proceeded to take one wine jug in her right hand, one in her left and departed. She soon returned from the cellar with both jugs filled to the brim with wine as the rejoicing continued.

The Deaf Man

The Baal Shem's grandson, Efraim tells how his grandfather had told him that a fiddler once played so well and so sweetly that everyone who heard him began to dance and whoever was near enough to hear would join in the dance. A deaf man came by while a crowd had begun to dance and it seemed to him that he was surrounded by madmen who had completely lost their sensibilities and were acting with poor taste.

Japanese

The Terrible Eek

One very stormy night, there was a family tucked into their little thatched house in the mountains. The father and son sat warming their hands over a small fire while the mother went about preparing their supper. The rain fell heavily on the little house and the strong winds shook its walls. The noises of the storm began to frighten the little boy and meekly he looked up at his father and asked, "Papa, are you ever afraid?"

"Oh yes, son, there are things which frighten me," nodded his father.

"What is it that frightens you most in the world?" asked the boy.

"Well, among humans, it is a thief that frightens me most," answered the father.

Now it just so happened that a thief was climbing on the roof of that very house, hoping to steal something on that dark and rainy night. When he heard the father's answer to his son's question he was filled with pride. "I am what they fear most in the world! How strong and powerful I am!"

The father continued to answer his son. "Among animals, I must say that I fear the wolf the most."

At that very moment there was a wolf creeping just under the window of the little house, hoping to steal a chicken for his dinner. Upon hearing the father's words he laughed proudly.

"I am what they fear most in the world! How strong and powerful I am!"

"But the most frightening thing of all," the father continued,"especially on a night like tonight, is a terrible leak. I truly hope there are no leaks tonight!"

The sounds of the wind and rain had grown quite loud, and the wolf strained to hear the father's words. "Did he say a terrible eek? Why, I've never heard of an eek before, but if it is what frightens him most of all it must be very fearsome indeed!" thought the wolf.

The thief high on the roof could barely hear the father's words between the gusts of wind. "Did he say he was afraid of a terrible eek?" wondered the thief. "I don't know what an eek is, but if it is what he fears most in the world it must be horrible!"

Just then, a great gust of wind knocked the thief over and he slid uncontrollably down the wet roof and landed with a thump right on the back of the wolf. The thief was so surprised to feel something wet and furry beneath him that he was certain that he had landed on an eek. And the wolf, surprised by the sudden burden on his back, thought surely it must be an eek gripping him tightly around the neck. With a great howl, the wolf began running with all his might through the trees while the thief clung with all his might to the wolf's back. The terrified wolf tore through the forest thinking, "Oh no! How will I ever get this eek off my back?" And the terrified thief thought as they sped along, "Oh no! How will I ever get off the back of this eek?"

Then all at once, the thief spied a low-hanging branch. He reached up and caught it as the wolf shot out from under him. But the branch was too weak to hold the thief, and it snapped and he fell. Now it just so happened that there was a deep hole right next to the tree and the thief fell into it. He tried to climb out, but it was too deep and the sides too slippery.

Meanwhile, the wolf, quite relieved to have the burden off his back ran back to his den. Quite breathless, he stopped at a stream to drink and there, he met a tiger. "What's the matter, Wolf?" inquired the tiger. You look as though you've had quite a fright."

"Oh yes, I have. I've just had the most terrible eek jump on my back. It gripped me by the neck and I ran and ran until finally, it let go."

"Why, I've never heard of a terrible eek in my life," laughed the tiger.

"Humans fear it more than anything," said the wolf, "and now I understand why. It is a terrible and fearsome thing."

"But I am the most powerful and fearsome creature that humans are afraid of!" cried the tiger. "I will find this terrible eek and catch him just to prove it!"

So the wolf and tiger set off into the forest. They had not gone far when they met a monkey. "What are you two doing at this time of night?" the monkey inquired.

"We're off to catch the terrible eek," replied the tiger.

"I've never heard of a terrible eek," said the monkey.

"It's the most fearsome creature in the world," said the wolf. "I know because there was one on my back not too long ago."

"I would like to see you catch this creature. I'm coming along," said monkey.

The wolf led the monkey and the tiger back to the tree where the thief had jumped off. They spotted the deep hole and wolf whispered, "I think it might be down there."

"Are you in there terrible eek?" roared the tiger. But there was no response. The thief was certain that the eek had come back to get him, and so he remained silent.

Winking at the others, the monkey said "I will lower my tail into the hole. The eek will grab onto it. You catch him as soon as he's out of the hole." The others nodded.

Slowly, the monkey lowered his furry tail into the hole. The thief grabbed onto the tail and pulled hard. The monkey became frightened and pulled back even harder, trying to recover his tail. But the thief held fast. The wolf pulled on the monkey, and the tiger pulled on the wolf with such force that the thief came flying out of the hole, letting out an enormous cry. The cry startled the monkey who screamed, "It's an eek!"

"Oh no, it's an eek!" cried the wolf, turning to the tiger.

"Oh no, an EEEEEEEEEEEEEK!" screeched the tiger.

"EEEEEEEEEEEEEEK!" hollered the thief.

All the noise and ruckus scared each one so much that they all ran off in different directions, each hoping that the eek was not following them.

Meanwhile, all snug in their little thatched house was the family preparing for bed.

"Goodnight, son," said the father.

"Goodnight, papa. It's a good thing there were no terrible leaks tonight," said the son.

"You're right, son," said the father. "There were no terrible leaks."

PROVERBS AND MAXIMS

You cannot prevent the birds of sorrow from flying over your head, but you can prevent them from building nests in your hair.
— *Chinese Proverb*

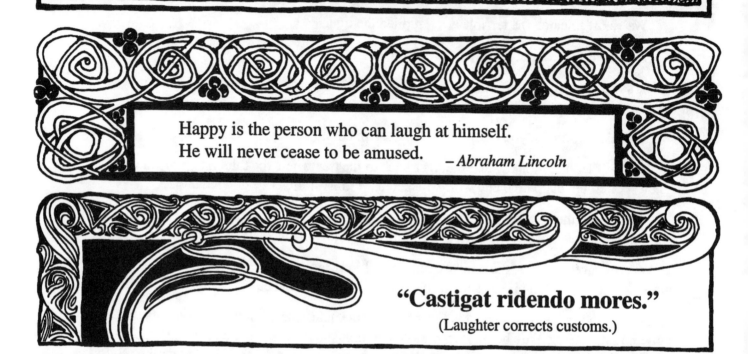

Happy is the person who can laugh at himself.
He will never cease to be amused.
— *Abraham Lincoln*

"Castigat ridendo mores."
(Laughter corrects customs.)

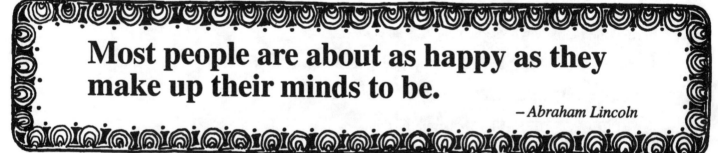

Most people are about as happy as they make up their minds to be.
— *Abraham Lincoln*

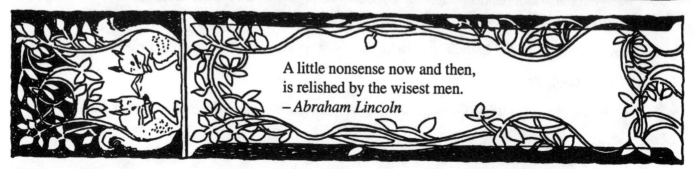

A little nonsense now and then,
is relished by the wisest men.
— *Abraham Lincoln*

HEROES AND HEROINES

LUCILLE BALL (1911–1989)

Born in Celeron, New York, a suburb of Jamestown near Lake Chautauqua, Lucille derived from her grandfather, a woodturner in a furniture factory, her instinct for family loyalty and for survival by hard work. As a child, she loved going to vaudeville shows and movies and then acting out what she had seen. She failed at a New York City dramatic school and was either fired from or not called for several shows. She worked as a soda jerk and a model before she became known as the Chesterfield Cigarette Girl, and had a chance for a movie role in 1933. Over the next few years and many bit parts in films, she recognized her strength in comedy and gradually increased her $50 a week salary to $3,500 a week. Her "universal language of wacky humor" and her irrepressible optimism finally paid off when the "I Love Lucy Show" premiered in 1951. It became one of TV's four all-time hits, and she was awarded the title "Comedienne of the Century" in 1964.

ERMA LOUISE FISTE BOMBECK (1927–1996)

Born in Dayton, Ohio, she has been described as a housewife turned humorist. She had the uncanny ability to take everyday occurrences and annoyances and, writing with wry humor, turn them into delightful anecdotes that helped Americans laugh at themselves. She graduated with a degree in English from the University of Dayton and began her writing career with the Journal Herald in Dayton, where she wrote obituaries and stories for the women's page. She married William Lawrence Bombeck in 1949 and put her writing aside when they adopted their first child in 1953. In 1964, she began writing a humor column, which was syndicated within weeks; at the peak of the column's success, her humor was enjoyed by a readership of 30 million people in over 900 newspapers. She wrote eleven books and made regular appearances on the "Good Morning America" show. She and her husband were generous members of their community and contributed many hours of volunteer work, especially with the American Red Cross.

BILL COSBY (1937–)

Born in the Germantown district of North Philadelphia, Pennsylvania as William Henry Cosby, Jr., he grew up in an all-black housing project. His father was a Navy mess steward and his mother worked as a domestic. His father was away a lot but his mother read to him regularly from the Bible and Mark Twain, teaching him to stay away from the dangers of the inner city ghetto. As a child, he was inspired by the comedian Sid Caesar and he earned the reputation of "an alert boy who would rather clown than study" (so writes a sixth-grade teacher). Bill dropped out of school in the tenth grade and joined the navy, where he earned a high school equivalency diploma. He went to college on a track and field scholarship at Temple University in Philadelphia, earning a degree in Physical Education. His career in comedy began in college when he took a part-time job tending bar and telling jokes in a Philadelphia coffeehouse, the Cellar. Today, Bill has a successful career as the dominant comedic voice of black Americans.

WILL ROGERS (1879–1935)

Born in his parents' ranch house between the Oklahoma towns of Claremore and Oologah, he was named William Penn Adair Rogers. His father, Clem, and mother, Mary, were part Cherokee and that part of Oklahoma was still Indian territory when he was born. Will was a very bright young boy and was offered an excellent education, but he wasn't interested in school and chose to speak with a Western drawl. He inherited his mother's easygoing manner and sense of humor. He became one of America's most loved characters and achieved great success as a philosopher, columnist, movie star, radio personality, and philanthropist. His humor poked fun at hypocrisy, smugness, and greed, even at the very famous. He did this with such genuine humor that everyone loved him. He loved to travel and wasn't afraid to take risks. His love of flying, when it was still dangerous, led to his early death. While on a flight around the world, he crashed with his good friend Wiley Post in Point Darrow, Alaska.

RED SKELTON (1913–1997)

Born in Vincennes, Indiana as Richard Bernard Skelton, he was the only redhead in the family and soon acquired the nickname that he was to adopt as his first name. He began his professional career at age ten, working as a medicine show singer, a tent-show performer, a circus clown, and a showboat comedian. He was the youngest of burlesque comedians at age sixteen. His formal schooling ended with the seventh grade when he left home to take up show business. He married Edna Stillwell when he was eighteen in 1931, struggled through the depression, and finally experienced some success in 1936. He was soon appearing regularly on the radio and making movies. He continued performing in clubs and comedy concerts through the 1980s. He also wrote music and did paintings of clown faces. He possessed broad antic talents of pantomime, mugging, and knockabout routines. He is well known for his characterizations of the Mean Widdle Kid, the mute hobo Freddie the Freeloader, and the simple-minded rustic Clem Kadiddlehopper.

MARK TWAIN (1835–1910)

Born in Florida, Missouri as Samuel Langhorne Clemens, he was the son of a storekeeper who was also at times a lawyer who struggled with success. Failure in business moved the Clemens family to Hannibal, Missouri, which became the hometown of Sam Clemens and the town that played significant roles in some of his finest work. His experiences in Hannibal as a boy, his work as a steamboat pilot and reporter on the western frontier, and his travels abroad provided him with the experiences and materials for most of his successful writing. He had very little formal education and his work varied in excellence because of his natural tendency to write intuitively and with improvisation. His successful novels charmed the American public because of their humor and their portrayal of the life and times of 19th Century America; *The Adventures of Tom Sawyer* (1876) and *The Adventures of Huckleberry Finn* (1884) will remain as American classics. His travels, his unique historical perspectives, and his tendency to speak his mind produced essays, articles, and humorous sketches about life in America. He launched another career as a humorous lecturer and enjoyed taking advantage of the foibles of politics and religion.

PUT HUMOR INTO ACTION

- Smile when you say "good morning."

- Laugh a little every day.

- Do something for someone that you know will make them happy.

- Be enthusiastic about something.

- Tell a joke.

- Listen to a joke.

- Read a funny story.

- Share a cartoon that you thought was funny.

- Laugh at yourself if you make a mistake or do something silly.

- Talk with people about the humor in life.

- Take moments to "lighten up"; be serious when necessary but don't take everything seriously, especially yourself.

COMMUNITY SERVICE IDEAS

- Rent a video of a comedy from the 40s and show it at a retirement home.

- Make placemats for a hospital decorated with cartoons and jokes.

- Organize a group of friends (or your soccer team, softball team, or scout troop) and put on a funny play for a children's hospital.

- Volunteer at a hospital to deliver mail or packages to patients with a big smile on your face.

- Work on a summer program with children.

- Cut-out and decorate lots of bookmarks from page 164. Dress-up as clowns and hand them out at a park, bank, or other public place.

- Organize a talent night at your school. Recruit volunteers from the community to perform.